WHAT WOULD WATER DO?

Simple Strategies for Navigating Life's Obstacles

BROOKE LENNON

DEDICATION

To the Loves of my Life:

Dear Husband, Baby Girl, Little Man, and Wee One.

You are my WHY

and I love you to the moon and back.

Thou

CONTENTS

BROOKE LENNON

ACKNOWLEDGEMENTS

Special thanks to the village that supported me throughout this entire adventure. I am deeply indebted first and foremost to all of the people throughout my life who listened to what I had to say. The ones who followed it up with, "That is soooo helpful – you really should write a book!" are the catalysts who sparked the idea for What Would Water Do? These are my past and present friends, teammates, colleagues, mentees, and the occasional random stranger who I came out of my introverted shell to meet. To those on my teams who became my test subjects throughout the years, thank you, I'm sorry, and you're welcome. Mostly, thank you.

These are your narratives, and I am grateful to have witnessed them in action. A special shout-out to Alicia, Althea, Benjamin, Cindy, Connor, Cynthia B., Cynthia M., Dave, David, Essie & Peter, Evelyn, Grace & Mike, Hari, Jeniffer, Jill & Doug, Joyce, Kelly, Kevin, Leigh, Patrick, Quincy, Shel, Sravanthi, Stacey, Tami, and Yana who graciously allowed me to use their names, words, and/or stories. Any errors or omissions are solely mine.

Keeping it real, I certainly did not invent a good portion of what I had to say to the lovely folks I worked with. I thank my own teachers, mentors, role models, colleagues, friends, and family for giving me this wisdom in the first place. These are the giants upon whose shoulders I stand. These are also your stories, and I thank you for shaping me into the person I am today. I hold each of you in the highest echelons of respect and honor.

In the creation of this edition, I owe a debt of gratitude to all who helped me take this from a collection of old blog posts to what you see today. Thank you to my early readers Cynthia B, Kelly, Mike, Matt, Alicia, Husband, and Mom who read it cover to cover at least twice in its painfully raw early versions. Mad respect to my talented editor Adrienne Horn at I A.M. Editing, Ink. She helped bring my vision to life with her word artistry. She also took my stories personally and experimented with some ideas to navigate through her own obstacles. I cannot express how much that meant to me. Lastly, I adore the cartoons that my illustrator Alifstyle created. They paint each scene with humor. I am astonished at how he was able to read my mind so clearly to tap into my concepts.

Lastly, I am indebted to my immediate family who gave me the support to bring this dream to reality. Many sections were researched, written, and/or edited while we were together. They gave me the time and space to have my head in my computer and away from each of them. Baby Girl decorated several of my original hardcopy drafts with doodles of foxes, puppies, and kitties while I worked. Little Man often benefitted from ten extra minutes after his sports practices ended for me to finish capturing my thoughts. He never minded the bonus time to keep kicking a ball, shooting hoops, or splashing in the pool. Wee One was a bit more active in the process, insisting on sitting on one knee or the other while I typed, asking to push the keys for me. These were not the most efficient of writing sessions to be fair. Finally the love of my life, Husband encouraged me, kicked me in the backside to keep going, and challenged me on my thought process at every step of the way. At the same time, he stayed out of the creative process to let me do this in my own unique style. Always my cheerleader, he helps turn my nos into yeses and pushes me to be the happiest me I can be. No words exist to express the depth of my appreciation and adoration.

INTRODUCTION: MY WISH FOR YOU

I wish for you to lead a life full of wild, raging success upon which you look back and laugh with giddy delight.

I wish you a life filled with more fulfillment, joy, happiness, and adventure than your craziest dreams ever envisioned. I wish you a life well lived in any of its manifestations, and the clarity of awareness to recognize your joy in the moment. It is my hope that you will pursue your passions with purpose.

I am a student of life and of people. Over my last two decades in Fortune 100 companies, I have led organizations ranging from two people to eleven hundred. I most love and embrace the leadership and personal development aspects of my job, both for the organizational whole and on a personal basis. In previewing my schedule each week, I most look forward to the deep one-on-one coaching and mentoring conversations with those on my team or who independently seek my counsel. The path to success is never without its speed bumps, and I love being able to help others navigate through the obstacles in their path.

This book thematically shares with you the individual conversations I regularly have. We all struggle with the same challenges, and I find myself frequently recounting the same stories. Some vignettes are my own; others feature friends and acquaintances. I include some favorite modern fables in my repertoire too. After receiving enough direct feedback on the value they provided, I was compelled to make my anecdotes more broadly available to others. I do not have all of life's great answers. I do possess an intense passion for growth and self-improvement. I love studying winners in life and what drives their success. Even they run into roadblocks; how they overcome these barriers time and time again is what sets them apart.

This word '*success*' means something different to each of us. For me, it includes travel and adventures, first as a soloist and now with my young family. To some, it means tackling momentous global issues like hunger, poverty, or disease so the world can be a better place. Others create a generational legacy, achieve fame and fortune, or amass and wield political power. Your purpose could be as profound as improving the life of a single person.

Success comes in all flavors, shapes, and sizes. There is neither a right nor wrong interpretation because *you* get to craft your own definition. Like beauty, it is in the eye of the beholder and the only beholder that matters *is you*! *Your* life, *your* game, *your* rules.

While each person may have a different definition, the common thread is that each one ignites passion and brings about purpose and joy. It gives you a deep sense of fulfillment in the present that is filled with both fond memories and anticipation of tomorrow's promise. Whether it is internally or externally oriented, public or private, large or small, one thing is for sure – it is all yours!

For me, success entails meeting and passing my time with interesting people, exposing myself to and exploring new ideas, and pushing myself beyond my preconceived limits to create joy, experience wonder, optimize my health, and build wealth.

Every strong organization has a purpose and a vision. Your life deserves no less. In 1998, the thought "I want to live a sparkly life" came to me while attending a seminar in Atlanta. Sparkly is the polar opposite of boring, and while hard to explicitly define for others, it became my personal mission statement.

I have since expanded my mission statement to "I want to live a sparkly life *with my family.*" Their presence in both the life and the sparkle is critical to my happiness. Sparkly for me *is* a measure of success. It is what I want to be when I grow up. It is what I want to reminisce about when I am old.

Do you know what *you* want to be when you grow up? What goals have you established for yourself and for your life? While it is okay to be unsure about what your master plan is going to be, you probably still want to achieve something of importance in the interim. How much daily progress do you make toward these goals? Little to none? What are you waiting for? Focus today on making the best use of your time. It is a non-renewable asset.

Take the time to design your own mission statement, even if it is temporary, while you figure out your master plan. Words matter and each one you choose must mean something to you. It can be conceptual or precise, as long as it provides you what you need to make choices and decisions in your life. For me, "I want to live a sparkly life with my family" is all I need to help me stay aligned to my North Star. You may choose to have a more elaborate and comprehensive manifesto.

Expect your success parameters to change over time. Your dreams and values will evolve and grow parallel with your WHY. Life will present you with wins and losses that adjust how you regard the world. It will force you to find your own place within it. You will create, reinforce, and redefine habits and behaviors that push you forward or hold you back.

Where you find yourself at any given moment will be a direct result of your thoughts and your actions coupled with the currents and boulders you encountered along your journey down the river of life. You can make progress even when you find yourself tossed about in whitewater or feel hopelessly stuck behind a rock. Remember, disappointments and setbacks are lessons. Once you embrace them for what they are, you will soon recognize your ability to guide yourself smoothly through life's course.

Are you living the life of your dreams? If your answer is "Not yet," relax. Perhaps you are stuck today, but that does not have to be permanent. We feel stuck when it seems we have no choices. Fortunately, you always have choices even when the situation *feels* hopeless. When faced with a roadblock, ask yourself, "What would water do?" As it courses down its riverbed, water encounters rocks and boulders in its path all the time. It may swirl around for a while, but ultimately it finds a way forward. Over, under, around or through – it keeps moving downstream. It finds the path of least resistance. You can too.

You *can* free yourself from the obstacles which hold you back. Perhaps some of these hit close to home:

- You find yourself living someone else's dream or you feel trapped at a dead end. You are not sure where you are going or why.
- The voices of your fears and doubts in your head drown out the dreams trying to get your attention. Your own beliefs are getting in your way.
- You know exactly what you want to do or whom you want to be but lack the time, money, knowledge or energy. You see your resource constraints limiting your potential.
- You know what you want to do, and you have rallied the necessary resources. You simply are overwhelmed.

At different points in my life, I have been stuck behind all four of these barriers. With the help of others, I found ways to press forward, time and time again. I endeavor to pay it forward through my stories. My goal is to help you live your own most rewarding life. Your dreams are within reach, and you have the power to make each one of them come to life.

I give you these pearls of wisdom to help you break through the difficult times you encounter while navigating your own river of life. I write this for all the younger Brookes out there whether or not I have had the opportunity to coach you personally.

I hope you find these ideas valuable while you seek your own destiny. Enjoy my vignettes, and when something resonates with you, commit to experimenting with at least three ideas that catch your imagination. Identify your dream, declare a major goal, and then set "micro-goals" to make progress one baby step at a time.

You can do it, I promise! DARE to overcome each of these obstacles with me:

Part 1: (D) Destination
> Assess your situation. Where are you now? What do you want your destiny to be?

Part 2: (A) Attitude
> Get your head into the right space, and obsess about what you can do, rather than what you cannot.

Part 3: (R) Resources
> Rally your resources. Assemble everything and everybody you need to set yourself up for success.

Part 4: (E) Execution
> Move past the thinking and onto the doing. Start small, take action, build momentum, and celebrate wins.

Life is but a dream, and we are meant to live it to its fullest capacity. Life is short yet wide with infinite possibility. We individually control our destinies in ways colossal and minute, with the opportunity to course correct at any time. It starts with a dream – *your dream* – and the will to take action. I *dare* you to be the most excellent version of yourself in all you undertake.

Thank you for inviting me into your story. Thank you for being a part of mine. Warmly,

Brooke "Brooxi" Lennon

PART 1: (D) DESTINATION

Destination   noun des·ti·na·tion \ ˌdes-tə-ˈnā-shən \ [1]

a place to which a person is going or something is being
sent

Word Origin: First known use 14th century

CHAPTER 1: THE TIES THAT BIND

Dear Brooke,

I finally know what I want to be when I grow up, but it's too late. I completed my schooling and got a good job with a great company. The pay is fine, and my family is so proud that I am making it on my own. They sacrificed so much for me to get here.

I could never disappoint them by throwing away all of my education and this job to chase my own dream now. I love them too much to hurt them in this way. All they want to know is that I'm set up for success. I'm stuck with this job, this degree, and this trajectory. I can see my entire future laid out ahead of me. Sigh.

DREAM YOUR OWN DREAMS, NOT MINE

To make your life meaningful, it must include your wildest dreams. Not my wildest dreams, not your dad's. Yours. While the list may include an array of items, your dreams are the big themes and achievements for your life. They may be public or private, professional or personal, large or small. They may skew toward the intellectual, the athletic, the political, the emotional, or the materialistic. Your dreams should be underpinned with aspects that give you fulfillment, which could come from any number of directions. With neither right nor wrong answers, common goals may include:

- Raising a family
- Starting a business
- Overcoming obstacles
- Giving back and helping others
- Pursuing academic discovery
- Physical fitness feats
- Immersing in your faith

The list is endless, bound by your own imagination and personal preferences. That which fulfills you may or may not fulfill me, and it does not need to. How do you recognize fulfillment? When you find yourself gaining satisfaction or joy from something even when you are not actively engaged with that activity or person. Tap into your own motivations. Do not get stuck living in somebody else's paradigm.

Some of us have known forever who or what we want to be and we pursue that with every fiber of our being. Not all of us are that blessed. Having spent time in both camps, I understand the feeling of crystal clarity on my dreams and goals as much as the feeling of being adrift. It manifests as uncertainty of what matters most, but still somehow manages to fill twenty-four hours each day without using it for a personally fulfilling purpose. Most children have grand aspirations. Once a young adult, the dreams begin to fade.

We realize we will not become a music star, professional ballplayer, or prima ballerina. The allure of becoming a firefighter peters out.

I ask from time to time what others plan to do when they retire. If they are nowhere near retirement, I inquire about what life they would live if money was no longer a factor and they could take care of their bills without having to work. In some ways, it amazes me how many people legitimately do not know what they would do with this most precious resource - time. In truth, for many years, I could not answer that question myself. Between second grade and my second job, I forgot how to dream and how to set goals for myself whose seeds were not sown by someone else.

My demise started when I stopped daydreaming. I actually got in trouble for it when I was in second grade. Mrs. Patterson wrote on my report card "Brooke daydreams too much" and "She needs to focus and get her head out of the clouds." I probably was just bored. Whether my own fault, Mrs. Patterson's, or the public school system's, I do not know. I gazed through the windows, thinking of everything I would rather be doing. My distraction caused no harm; my grades were fine. Sadly, I traded adventuring in my mind for putting my head down and focusing. I followed instructions and eventually stopped asking myself where I would rather be.

I certainly am not alone. Researchers asked dying hospice patients to share their greatest regrets. Besides the expected "I wish I worked less," which came in second, the number one response was wishing they had lived and pursued their own life's dreams, and not somebody else's.

Consider this classic American story, where the parents set a course for a beloved child's success. In dogged pursuit of this future vision, the child earns straight As and is accepted into a series of Ivy League schools. Ultimately, the child becomes a doctor or lawyer with a loaded bank account, flashy car, and a big house in a prestigious zip code. This is often accompanied by large debts that create sticky financial barriers when they desire to change course later on. Children feel the pressure to perform and to live up to these expectations. They either shelve their own dreams or never pause to figure out for themselves who or what they could be. Indeed, we are seeing young adults put themselves under greater amounts of pressure than prior generations, striving for this golden dream that many never asked for or aspired to.

Top 5 Regrets of Hospice Patients[2]

1. **I wish I'd had the courage to live a life true to myself, not the life others expected of me.**
2. I wish I hadn't worked so hard.
3. I wish I'd had the courage to express my feelings.
4. I wish I had stayed in touch with my friends.
5. I wish I had let myself be happier.

Nobody is at fault. Parents wish success and self-sufficiency for their children after they leave the nest. Children want to please the most important adults in their world. I call out no bad dogs here, but I observe a fundamental problem. The dreams belong to the dream creators - not to their offspring.

My own mother crushed my GrampO's dreams for her when she married my dad before their senior year of college. They were in love and intended to enjoy a year of married life before he was slated to head to the Vietnam War upon graduation. GrampO had dreams of Mom spending three months traveling Europe between graduation and grad school. Being natives of the Pacific Northwest, he looked forward to her meeting and marrying an engineer from Boeing. Mom had no idea that these were his dreams for her. When she proceeded to marry Dad anyway, Grama had to intervene to restore peace within the family. It was a mess.

While Mom followed her own path early on, I am a textbook example of following the path that was implicitly laid out for me. I succeeded in school because I naturally have always had the inclination to strive for top marks. Maybe this stems from Precious Firstborn Syndrome. Perhaps I was wired this way in utero. Regardless, I took the hardest classes early on, including advanced mathematics, and was accepted into excellent schools. After graduation, I joined prestigious programs at one of the most admired companies in the world. I won the highest awards and honors and was promoted many times. Money was earned, invested, and saved. I could measure my success by title, salary, bank account balances, and all that I owned. Yay me! Deep sigh. Unfortunately, the fulfillment was missing from these accomplishments. I was not pursuing my dreams because I had no idea what they were.

If you have not yet taken the time to watch Randy Pausch's *The Last Lecture: Achieving Your Childhood Dreams*,[3] make it a point to watch it on YouTube. Randy was a highly respected and beloved professor of Computer Science at Carnegie Mellon University. CMU hosted a lecture series where academics prepared and delivered talks as if it was their final lecture on earth. For Prof. Pausch, it tragically was. He was fighting through the last few months of pancreatic cancer. He spoke of accomplishing his own childhood dreams and empowering others to do the same. After a decade, it still sticks with me.

Randy notes, "Experience is what you get when you didn't get what you wanted." Surely you have heard or said to another, "I didn't enjoy [XYZ], but it was a good experience." There is deep truth to this. You **are** getting valuable experience in everything new you do regardless of whether or not you enjoy it. You never know when a bad experience may open a door or prepare you for a phenomenal opportunity later in life. Certainly, a collection of experiences (good, bad, and ugly) can take you farther than a collection of good experiences alone. As my buddy Quincy says, "Experience is what you get two minutes after you needed it."

Experience builds you up and forms a critical part of your education. I would simply suggest if you are getting an education *formally or informally*, be sure to pursue a major in a topic you love.

"I'm a big fan of 'if what you're doing hurts, stop doing it!'"

~ Althea Martelino, friend

MY KILLER JOB WAS KILLING ME

For three years, I held a job chock full of, "No, I do not like my work, but I am learning a lot and I am gaining great experience" moments. One day it dawned on me that the world has infinite possibilities of great (and lousy) experiences, but I have finite time on this earth. Yes, I am learning a lot, but are these the experiences I want to accumulate?" I thought I was stuck, but my own thoughts kept me there. I had a choice, and the choice I was making was to tough it out.

Was I always happy? Well … I do not know if I ever stopped to ask myself this. I was on my path and making measurable progress. That was success, right? By my parents' assessment, I could not have been doing much better. By my own though? I was unsure of how to gauge success.

I recall taking a late night cross-country flight heading east from California to Washington, DC. I always choose left-side window seats because they are the easiest for me to sleep in. Before nodding off that time, I read the back section of my alumni magazine where classmates write in with updates on what they have been up to since we last met. One was curing cancer, someone else was creating clean water supplies in an undeveloped country, and a third was doing something mind-blowing with micro-electronics.

I stared at my reflection in the oval window. I was a world traveling, fast-rising corporate auditor in a prestigious company's premier leadership development program. Big whoop. The work was unrelated to anything I had ever dreamed about, and in the grand scheme of things, I was not sure it even mattered. Was this the full manifestation of my life's purpose? In truth, it depressed me while I stared out of the tiny window at the illuminated landscape below.

Although the tangible rewards were rich and the all-expense paid world travel was incredible, I derived little personal satisfaction from the work I invested my life into. I felt stuck in the race to the top of the corporate ladder, giving every ounce of myself to the climb. Furthermore, being unmarried and without children, I created no boundaries. I devoted an obscene number of hours of my day to work. For what? No matter how much love or loyalty I could give to a company, that company would never love me back. No company can. While being composed of humans, the company itself is inanimate.

What was depressing soon became soul crushing when I asked myself what I should be doing to find fulfillment. I drew a blank. Nothing I was doing seemed worthy of a life's work. Nothing got me particularly excited. I felt a huge void. I was clueless about what I wanted to do. You can always ask the hypothetical, "If you won the lottery, did not need an income, and could do anything, what would it be?" I had no idea and it made me sad. For years, instead of pausing to figure it out, I kept doing what I was doing to avoid thinking about it. Sound familiar?

Ultimately I decided that this seemingly glamorous jet-setting life was not making me happy. Trying to date around a heavy travel schedule was virtually impossible and I missed having the comforts of a home with a bed of my own. I worked too much and kept working even while my body sent me warning signals

through pre-ulceric acid reflux and exhaustion. My killer job was killing me. Despite enviable locations, the inside of a conference room looks and feels pretty much the same worldwide. The offices in Paris and Tokyo happen to be smokier. I realized I needed to spend my time and energy on areas I am the most passionate about.

Follow YOUR passions and get good and bad experiences THERE. Avoid being an expert in something you hate, to avoid feeling stuck in that area forever. If you dream of being a masseuse, getting your accounting degree may not be the best use of your time. Yes, accounting is a great skill to acquire, and yes, you WILL LEARN A LOT. However, it does not get you closer to your massage license. Unless accounting is how you are planning to pay the bills while you are getting your spa off the ground (i.e., a means to an end), or you need it to manage the business side of your spa, it will be a waste of your time. If you hate numbers, expect pain. Go to your happy massage place; I guarantee you will find plenty of bad experiences there too, but at least they will be on the journey to reaching your ultimate destination.

As you accumulate "bad" experience along the way, try to learn something different from each situation. There is good to be found in non-favorable experiences, and variety is the key. Getting hit by the same stick over and over again gives you the same bad experience over and over. You can only learn so much from the same experience. Let negative experiences motivate you to make a positive change because you are worth it.

"I'm glad I did it, partly because it was worth it,
but mostly because I shall never have to do it again"

~ Mark Twain, American Author

CHAPTER 2: STARING INTO THE VOID

Dear Brooke,

All this talk of dreams, quite frankly, depresses me. I have NO IDEA what I want to do with my life, or what my purpose on this planet is. Everyone else around me seems to be working toward something, but when I ask myself what my "something" is, all I hear is radio silence. I'm stuck doing what I'm doing on autopilot because what on earth would I do instead? How on earth do I figure it out? Am I defective?

STILL A VOID

A life of fulfillment is waiting for you. We simply need to find out what is missing.

In my coaching business, it saddens me when clients cannot articulate dreams of their own nor recognize this to be a concern. Generally, when I start an engagement, I try to understand the whole person I am working with prior to digging into any specific topics. Understanding an individual's context precedes trying to help him or her work through whatever facet they wish to develop. I had two sessions within a few days of one another that particularly struck me.

The first woman sought me out for help to work through general career development concerns. She knows she would rather be restoring art over ensuring banking compliance but wrote it off as too unprofitable to maintain her family's finances. She has relegated her dream and passion to "Someday Isle" or "Not Gonna Happen Bay" because she still must resolve the fiscal speed bump. Unfortunately, it has become a roadblock instead of a speed bump, and there it remains for the foreseeable future. Unless something dramatic changes, the goal is on hold until she reaches empty nest status.

A second woman approached me for help with remote communication. Working in different offices, we regularly engage in video and phone conferences, and she wants to be as effective as possible in both formats. In our introductory conversations, I probed to understand the course of her career. She and I were both proud of and excited about her recent promotion, for which she worked incredibly hard. I wanted to know what was next for her in terms of her new goal and next career milestone. In short (though seasoned in her career), I was curious to know who she wanted to be when she grew up?

She struggled to articulate anything concrete, speaking words about wanting to help people and make a difference. I encouraged her to take it another step further, because countless paths allow her to help people and make a difference. She either could not or would not. I know how undeniably scary staring into that void is. I have compassion for her because I vividly recall that feeling myself.

Unfortunately, this is more common than not. I am a member of an online forum centered on motivation and goal achievement. One member's post was incredibly simple and profoundly sad.

> ### How do I figure out my own dreams?

Many comments followed her post, empathizing and sharing similar frustrations. It seems to be an epidemic, this undreaming state. Having been there myself at another time and place, I feel her void.

This is what helps me, and it is the comment I posted for her. I believe your dreams are hiding within your heart and waiting to be coaxed out. Think about what you are doing when you are at your happiest. Listen to yourself whenever the words, "I wish …", "I want … ", or "I would love …" escape your lips. What comes after those words? If the answers are broad or vague, ask yourself what the deeper manifestation is, and what that might look like if it came to fruition. If this is all too optimistic for your current thinking, consider the opposite of what keeps you up at night worrying, or when you are in your times of deepest despair. Do you have financial woes? Are you lonely or afraid? Do you miss somebody deeply? What would the polar opposite situation be?

Think about what activities give you the deepest sense of fulfillment. Is it when you are surrounded by specific people or certain types of people? Is it when you are working on a meaningful project at work? Does fulfillment derive from your place of worship or its community? What makes you FEEL GOOD in a natural state, meaning when alcohol or other external substances are not shifting your chemical balance? Once you have identified one or more activities to get started, look for underlying themes you could extrapolate and magnify.

Do you wish for a dream job or a dream house? A better life for your children? Escape from a terrible situation? A deep relationship with a wonderful life partner? Financial freedom? Adventure? Peace and quiet? All of the above?

If you do not know or care where you are going, it does not matter how hard or fast you row your boat. Indeed, it does not matter if you row at all. Spend quality time with yourself figuring out where you wish to go.

"Alice: Would you tell me, please, which way I ought to go from here?
The Cheshire Cat: That depends a good deal on where you want to get to.
Alice: I don't much care where.
The Cheshire Cat: Then it doesn't much matter which way you go."

~ Lewis Carroll, Alice in Wonderland[4]

IDENTIFY YOUR WHY

It is so much easier said than done to simply "figure out your dreams." I get it. Consider some proven techniques to start figuring it out. I find it helpful to identify and hone in on your WHY as a starting point. Knowing and acknowledging what is most important to you is often the key to discovering self-fulfillment, where your dreams are most vivid.

The autumn foliage of 2015 was particularly breathtaking in central Virginia. I have no idea precisely when the fall colors started emerging, but I feel they lasted for a solid four weeks. New electric reds and radiant orange hues covered the trees and later the streets once they fell. I cannot recall a prettier autumn. Each morning while driving up the highway to work, it hit me again. After remarking to myself how lovely it all was, I reminded myself of its temporary nature. Soon it would fade to memory, which also diminishes over time. Being yet another reminder to live in and cherish the present, I took a moment to simply breathe, look, and enjoy. Life is fleeting, and we live only in the present, though most of us try to hold on to the past while worrying about the future.

I remind myself to do that when I am with my three little ones too. They will be small for such an achingly short time. Soon they will neither demand nor want my help in getting dressed or holding their small hands when we come down the stairs. Infinite hugs and kisses when I leave the house in the morning, or their requested "hundred million" more at bedtime have already started fading away. In a few years they will not want their friends to see me when they get dropped off for school or athletic events. For now, I remind myself: breathe, smile, and rejoice in their unconditional love for you. This moment will be a memory in a blink of an eye.

I share this vivid memory because my children and their father form the center of my world. They are my highest priority right now, and I carve out sizeable blocks of time for them. They are my WHY. When I want to give up because of whatever is standing in my way, they keep me going. When I am driving down the highway and feel the tug to keep on driving to see where the road ends, they are the reason I take the exit toward home. When I am wanting to park on the couch with a fork and a whole pie, they are the ones who inspire me to take a walk instead. I need to be healthy for me, but I also want to be healthy so I may enjoy every minute of the remainder of my life with them.

Interestingly, I use them for guidance, to remind myself to live the healthiest life I can and how I should behave. They are my judges and jury. Though a five-year-old is pretty darn forgiving today, fifteen and twenty-five-year-olds are much less so. How will they judge me as a mother and a person? Am I living my life as a positive example as a woman and a human being? Do I treat others in the way I want my children to treat others and to be treated in return? I wish to live my life as a role model, fully knowing that while they are not consciously watching me, everything I do and say will somehow be repeated by them later. "For better or for worse" applies to parenting in parallel to marriage, but in different ways. My children will become mini-mes as they mature... for better or for worse. My job is to be the best me I can be for them. They drive me forward. While my life is by all accounts comfortable, having a WHY is a basic survival need.

In his heart-wrenching book, *Man's Search for Meaning*[5], Dr. Viktor Frankl explores that which drives people to keep on going in the most brutal and hopeless of circumstances. Dr. Frankl survived not just Auschwitz but also two Dachau-affiliated Nazi Concentration Camps in World War II. His insights while imprisoned informed his life's work thereafter. He observed that people with a reason to live survived despite the worst conceivable circumstances. Those who gave up or lost their will to live subsequently died soon thereafter.

Dr. Frankl cited three themes for this will, in the form of how meaning is derived:

For some, it was one or more people that they had to survive for. **Love** drove their resolve and powered them through another day in the innermost circle of hell.

For others, their will is powered by a higher order, where their faith prohibits suicide and, in this context, giving up. They found meaning in **suffering**, and rose above it in a most personal and profound way. While they could not change their situations, they were able to change their reactions and attitudes. This made all the difference.

Then there were those whose survival was centered around a life's **calling**, or a body of work that had to be accomplished to fulfill one's destiny. Perhaps this was an interrupted project, or one not yet begun at the point of imprisonment.

When the pull from one or more of these WHYs is strong enough, individuals live against all odds of starvation and torture and thrive despite lesser types of obstacles.

When your WHY is visceral and you live your life in accordance with the values that accompany it, you set yourself up for abundance, joy, and fulfillment. Knowing what matters most to you and aligning your actions accordingly makes most decisions easier.

"Those who have a 'why' to live, can bear with almost any 'how.'"

~ Friedrich Wilhelm Nietzsche, German philosopher

BABY GIRL DOESN'T CARE

Husband started a company five years ago. Routinely, he runs into people who try to take advantage of him and of what he does. A kind man, he characteristically seeks out the win-win in every situation. He is improving our region's affordable housing options one property at a time by providing property rentals and renovations for future residents. He finds himself being bombarded by residents who consider paying their agreed-upon rent optional, and contractors who choose not to show up on time or perform an honest day's work for an honest day's pay. People steal tools and materials from him, violate their contracts, and take advantage of his kindness. There is always an excuse that pushes his compassion and understanding to the limit.

After enough people tried to take advantage of him, he drew the line. The company is our family's financial future, and he had to do what was right to ensure its success. He coined the mantra "Baby

Girl doesn't care" to remind himself of his WHY for when he needed guidance on how to proceed. If we fail to collect the rental income, we cannot pay the mortgages. We may lose the properties or be unable to buy groceries or put our children in extracurricular activities.

Our older daughter, "Baby Girl," is now eight years old. She neither understands nor cares about all the reasons why the business lacks the revenues it requires due to others' excuses or failings. She simply knows whether or not she can take the art class she loves.

This does not mean Husband is without understanding or compassion, or that he ignores the big picture. He gets it! It simply means that when faced with a decision, the litmus tests of what does it mean to our eight-year-old and her long-term happiness makes all the difference.

This test can be taken to a more strategic level. When Husband decides where to invest himself, he needs to manage how much he takes on at any given time. At some point, if she never gets to see her daddy, Baby Girl also does not care about that hundredth art class she will never take anyway. For us, our family is our WHY. Part of our roadmap is reaching a state of financial freedom so we can share incredible experiences in the present and the future.

Our health goals tie into this too. Baby Girl does not care for my excuses when I get inadequate rest after staying up too late and then feel too tired to get up and exercise my body or discipline myself to eat properly. If I am not rested and my temper is short, or I cannot keep up physically with her and her siblings, she disregards any excuse I drum up. She knows what it means to her and she is not interested in any flimsy justification I offer. We can learn volumes from our children. They are my family's foremost WHY, as is the case for most parents.

A second lesson in knowing our WHY comes from Mike and Grace, who are entering the next season of their lives. Their children are both well-educated adults, who live the twenty-something lifestyle. Mike and Grace have a nice portfolio of assets and they are virtually debt-free. They have reached a point of financial freedom where their time is more valuable to them than their money. They have enough financial security to live the rest of their lives in the style of their choosing. They shared that they need to focus on maximizing time instead of money.

We talked over drinks while Mike debated getting involved with all the new automation techniques and technologies emerging in his industry. He was torn between committing to grow the business, including hiring employees and developing systems, or not. From an outside-looking-in point of view, it was unclear what problem he was seeking to solve.

In conversation, we challenged them to articulate their WHY. With financial security in hand, adding hassle seemed counter-intuitive to the statement that their time was of the utmost importance to them.

Mike contemplated his response. His answer resided some-where between being a serial entrepreneur, where the challenge of the game is the reward in and of itself, and with wanting to keep up with the newer generation coming into its own. This was where he found fulfillment, which is paramount.

His next step was to decide where his time would be spent best, what type of challenges would get his blood boiling the hottest, and how he could maximize the fulfillment he acquires out of using his time without driving Grace crazy. They were at a unique spot where they could do anything they wanted with their futures. Once Mike and Grace articulated their WHY for getting more involved in building their business during that season of their lives, it became easier for them to decide where to channel their energies.

How do you articulate your WHY? What propels you to get up in the morning? Everything we do or choose not to do is a reflection of our inherent values, whether we recognize it or not. This is an interesting conundrum when we pause to check for alignment. Let me share my own personal ah-ha moment.

When I first entered the workforce, I joined a wonderful entry-level technical leadership program. As part of our curriculum, we had a class where the instructor handed out stacks of little blue cards, each printed with a different value on it. The assignment was to prioritize what most contributed to my feelings of fulfillment.

We were instructed to put them in order of importance. I debated the sequence on a few, but it was a straightforward exercise. Family and friends were at the top, followed by my health, career advancement, making money, and being recognized. I am confident of this twenty-three years later only because I made a small note of the sequence on each card for future reference.

This distressed me when I gave myself a hard reality check. Society and families can pressure us to do or be a lot. I had to be honest with myself about whether my order reflected my actual values vs. what I thought they ought to be. I ranked family among my top three, but I lived in the California Bay Area alone while my immediate family resided in the suburbs of Washington, DC. Much of my extended family resided in the state of Washington. I made sporadic efforts to call and email them. It begs the question - was my family actually a top priority, or was "family" the conditioned response to what I thought my first priority *should* be?

The same realization applied to my health. While at the top of my stack ranking, I irregularly exercised, seldom watched my diet, and never slept enough. I enjoyed the life of a young professional in Silicon Valley, meeting and hanging out with friends, traveling the world for work, and enjoying newfound money. Clearly, there was very little healthy or family oriented about it.

I share this story because in order to discover our WHY, we need to examine both our stated and actual behaviors. Nothing is wrong with the life I loved in California. Truthfully, I would do it again. What I wish I had done sooner was be honest with myself so that I could have aligned my thinking with my doing. I lived more accidentally than on purpose. A very good life could have been a great life. I could have been and done more had I aligned myself in

Value Sort Cards

Family	Wealth	Power, Influence, Authority
Fame	Friendships, Social	Giving Back, Helping Others
Health, Physical Well-being	Career Advancement, Title	Recognition, Appreciation
Self-Realization	Travel and Adventure	Security
Alignment to Greater Purpose, Mission	Continued Learning, Development, Growth	Respect
Independence, Self-direction, Flexibility, Freedom	Fun, Laughter	Accomplishment + New Challenges

that way. I could have made fewer boneheaded mistakes and reduced the angst I experienced in the typical twenty-something fashion. Of course, hindsight sports 20/20 vision.

Since we are exactly where we are supposed to be based on all we have and have not done life-to-date, I recognize the opportunity to improve the outcomes by adjusting the inputs. I still have these little blue cards, and every few years I shuffle them up and sort them by my values in accordance with how I believe I live them. Each time I flip over each card to add the new date and sequencing.

It fascinates me to see what has changed and what has endured. Family monopolizes the top now, having married my best friend and added three little ones to the mix. We have the family business and our lives are full of school work, youth sports, sibling rivalry, and glitter. I value spending time with my family, building wealth to support its immediate and future needs, and optimizing our health so the ride along the way is fulfilling and flat-out fun.

What is your WHY? Think past your public values of what you might answer if an acquaintance casually asked you, and examine how you spend your resources. Where does your time, money, energy, and mindshare go most regularly? What gets you up onto your soapbox, or down into the pits of despair?

While we judge ourselves on intentions, others judge us by our actions. Sometimes those casual acquaintances and our friends can tell us more about ourselves than we know or are willing to acknowledge. If you ask ten people – friends, family, co-workers, acquaintances – who you are and what you stand for, would you be surprised by their answers?

What do your actions tell you about you? Do you like the picture it paints? If yes, magnify those actions. If no, it is time to adjust.

"Values are like fingerprints.
Nobody's are the same, but you leave 'em all over everything you do"

~ Elvis Presley, American singer, musician and actor

NEW DREAMS

I began moving past my own dreamless hurdle upon reading the fantastic *The Four Hour Workweek*[6]. This marvelous book made me think along the lines of "If I legitimately could stop working next year, what would I do?" This sounds incredibly cliché and it is. Being able to answer this question and make forward progress toward bringing those answers to life is mind-blowing. It is anything but cliché.

In *The Four Hour Workweek*, Tim Ferriss describes lifestyle engineering by this simple formula:

1. Create sufficient passive income requiring no more than four hours of nurturing each week.
2. Leverage automation, outsourcing, and empowerment
3. Shed the twenty percent of stuff sucking up eighty percent of your resources.
4. Go live life to the fullest.

Write a book, invest smartly, own real estate, create a company, and let others run your business for you. Shed the things that disinterest you, outsource everything you can, and focus on that which stirs your blood. Simple, right?

I started asking myself these questions for real. Once I removed the mental speed bump of "but I have to work to support the family," and combined it with "gosh this COULD become a possibility in the next few years," the dreams came at me fast and furious. I would spend time raising my kids before they get too old to want me around, do more yoga and outdoor cardio, plant and tend my garden, publish ten books, and enroll in culinary school. Heck, I might become a lunch lady at a downtown school, where I could affect a small daily difference for every kid who passed through my lunch line.

I contemplate starting a not-for-profit food truck delivery system to provide breakfast to hungry, underprivileged kids before school.

This combines my love for food, my obsession with combating our broken food system, my compassion for children, and belief in the power of education all in one. I have never been overly civic-minded in the past, but this idea came out of left field and resonated deeply. I articulate my idea to anyone who wants to know about it and their feedback helps evolve my thoughts into actionable plans.

I have toyed for years with running a catering business, accompanied by hard work and brutal hours. I plan to take cooking classes and maybe enroll in formal culinary school. Maybe I will formalize the cookbook I have been compiling for thirty years and publish it for others to enjoy.

The thought has crossed my mind to get involved politically to combat the disaster our food supply faces. Our country is overfed, yet undernourished. The United States has gone down such a slippery slope of bad health decisions, and someone must help claw us back. One of the stories I have always had for myself is *I hate politics...* but if politics entail making a difference through influence and partnership, maybe I should give it a go. What is the worst that might happen? Seems like a fair risk and one I need to contemplate.

I may also attend the local community college to learn how to program apps or teach myself the Python programming language under the tutelage of Prof. Google. I loved the undergraduate C programming class I aced, then failed to use for anything. Many times I have come up with ideas for apps or programs I would love to design. I hold back because I do not want to pay someone else to code them, putting my perceived intellectual property at risk. In my mind, I am not yet a computer programmer, but a small part of me wants to be. To heck with the Ivy League, this is for me, not my resume. I lack any desire to be a coder for some company. I want to create apps for my own amusement. If I can sell them great - more passive income for my family - but I am doing this for me.

My family thinks I have gone a wee bit loco, but they love me for it. I amuse them with my progressive ideas on farming and micro nutrition and my stories from the office. They have been wildly supportive as I continue refining these ideas. Although my current homeowner association forbids the laying hens I covet, both the sane and crazy ideas abound. I feel vibrant when I inhabit the "what if" headspace. That vitality translates into everything else I do throughout my day. Once I got past being stuck on the question of what I wanted to do, I started moving into tackling the questions of how can I do it and when.

My epiphany was that the adventures can start now, meaning today. Yours can too. By rearranging how we spend time, we can advance many of our objectives while holding down normal day jobs. I could have started any of them a decade ago. I could have lived inexpensively to stretch the savings while pursuing any of these dreams. However, it took me this long to figure out what my dreams are. Once we identify and prioritize our Big Rocks (more on these later!), we will find ourselves on the most amazing journeys. It starts with creating the time to accomplish the goals that are significant to us.

"If you can dream it, you can do it. Always remember that this whole thing was started with a dream and a mouse."

~ Walt Disney, Entrepreneur, Film Producer, Animator, Actor, and Visionary

KICK YOUR BUCKET LIST

We are far from done. Both your life and mine have a lot more success to offer in all its manifestations. For the first action challenge, I encourage you to create your Success Bucket List without any regard to your age. A Bucket List is a collection of experiences you wish to have before you "kick the bucket" (die), and of which you make a point of doing. The second half of that definition is important. Otherwise, you just have a dreamy piece of useless paper. Everyone should maintain a Bucket List, whether short-term or life-long. You should write down your dreams large and small, short-term and long-term, mundane and crazy.

My first Bucket List originated at the beginning of my senior year of college. It was handwritten in crayon. Knowing I would soon leave the Boston area, my friends and I captured all the things we wanted to do together before scattering to the four winds. While a few line items went undone, we had a fabulous time working through our list. Its mere existence was indeed the catalyst for the memorable outings we might not otherwise have thought to do when faced with an unscheduled Friday night. From riding all of Boston's T (subway) lines to each of their ends for the steep price of 85¢, to breaking through locked doors to climb on top of the great dome of MIT, we kept ourselves busy.

The Boston list had a finite expiration date that coincided with graduation. We knew we had to get it done or forgo the adventures forever. Even at that age, we realized we had to make it happen then and there. We could never recreate the circumstances to have the whole crew there together in the same single, freewheeling, broke circumstances that bound us. It was magnificent.

My more comprehensive lifelong Bucket List started in earnest in the late autumn of 2002 at the five-star Hilton Grand Hotel in New Delhi. After all these years, I relive the beauty of the hotel, with polished decor and manicured gardens, juxtaposed with the dusty brown, unpaved poverty three feet off the property line. A family prepared its morning meal over a small open fire at the side of the road where we passed through the gates. It made for a jarring transition into reality each morning. While lounging in the coffee shop sipping a cup of hot tea with milk, I contemplated my plans for the day. For my own safety as a young American woman, my hosts forbade me from venturing out of the hotel unescorted. In essence, I was stuck - trapped in this gorgeous, black marble cage on that sunny Sunday afternoon.

SCUBA diving initiated my Bucket List, ironically its absence rather than its presence. I was on an assignment in Asia for a third of the year. The company authorized a monthly all-expense paid weekend home or alternately local trips of equal or less cost. Several people took the opportunity when traveling to try their hands at diving, particularly when stationed within reasonable travel distance to Australia's Great Barrier Reef or other similar renowned diving spots.

While trying to plan out my next trip, I briefly considered SCUBA diving with the reflective "maybe another time." In that moment, I paused and asked myself, "Will there ever be 'that time'?" Furthermore, did I want to SCUBA for real, or was that what everyone else wanted to do and I felt I ought to? I realized that in actuality it ranked toward the bottom of my to-do list. It has taken me a lifetime, but I finally have internalized that knowing what you do not want counts as much as knowing what you do want. I wish I had internalized that truth twenty years earlier... or more accurately, had not forgotten it repeatedly. I realized it was time to start creating a legitimate Bucket List.

Onto my list went getting married, having kids, riding an elephant, and milking a cow. I want to perform something on stage and see Madonna in concert. I chose the arbitrary figure of creating a net worth of ten million dollars as an imprecise *freedom number*. It began to quantify the point where I could do or buy almost anything without having to check the bank account balance first. Whether the number is one, five, or fifty million matters less than visualizing what it means for my family and me. I intend to photograph Denali National Park and to visit every continent. I must witness the Aurora Borealis before I die. I will live in another country for real (not for work) while my children are still young and impressionable. I may try my hand at the World Series of Poker in Las Vegas. I intend to fit into size six jeans once more.

Notably, skydiving is off my list. I can go my entire life without jumping out of a functional airplane. I am neutral on SCUBA diving; if the opportunity presents itself, I may do it, but I will not go out of my way. I prefer to learn to surf and ride the waves of the Pacific Coast with one or more of my children. They experienced boogie boarding for the first time in the summer of 2016, and I believe I may have some future surfing buddies.

Furthermore, I have had experiences I can live with never repeating for one reason or another. I dated some people I should not have, and for much longer than wise. After sixteen weeks of living in India, I do not feel compelled to return. Twice I have auditioned for TV shows. I survived the online dating scene and participated in drunken bicycle rickshaw races through the midnight streets of Kathmandu during a weekend of civil unrest. I fed my little sister cat food, ate live sushi, did the body piercing thing several times, climbed up precarious rooftops, and wrecked a car on black ice. I also hurt people I love in various ways, and crippled relationships I should have cared for with all my heart. I hope I have adequately apologized and made my amends. Sometimes you win, sometimes you crash and burn. Sometimes you are just a big dummy. Hopefully, you always learn and avoid repeating your less prudent decisions.

Despite some of my less than stellar moments, I am thrilled and grateful for the opportunity and the courage to have experienced my life's adventures to date. Being able to articulate what you do and do not want is a critical input for your Bucket List. It should include goals, people, places, and things you want to experience, learn, and achieve. Your list should always be fluid and in edit mode. Hopefully, you will start crossing off line items, adding new ideas and deleting others that no longer hold appeal. While I want you always to be safe in life and limb, I hope you will take chances and have fun too. Life is but a dream. Make yours incredible!

"Happiness cannot be traveled to, owned, earned, worn or consumed.
Happiness is the spiritual experience
of living every minute with love, grace, and gratitude."

~ Denis Waitley, American motivational speaker and author

CHAPTER 3: SOMEDAY ISLE

Dear Brooke,

I have dreams, but I am nowhere near realizing them. I have known what I want to be since I was a child. For now I'm stuck with the life I know. My family needs all of my time, attention, and income, and I cannot let them down … I love them and take my responsibilities extremely seriously. Someday I'll pursue my personal destiny, but now is not the time. What can I do?

THE PRESENT OF TIME

How you manage your time does not merely correlate with success, but it is directly causal to it. If you squander time on activities that do not advance your priorities, they will be unhonored and unachieved indefinitely. To live an amazing, fulfilling, wildly successful life, we must apply meaningful amounts of time toward these goals. We cannot put them off until "someday" because all we have is today and today alone.

I find the concept of the present to be quite the enigma. Infinitely brief, it fills the instant trapped between past and future. The past is behind us, never to return or be modified no matter how we cling to it. The future is always beyond our grasp, never to be reached. One second ago was the past. One second from now is the future. The present is excruciatingly slim. Past and future happiness lives only in our minds. We have only present happiness to affect. Paradoxically and simultaneously, we experience the present every second of every day of our lives. With this vantage point, the present is infinite. Contradictions aside, if we are to accomplish anything at all, we have only this present moment to do it in. Use this time wisely.

If we are lucky, we have no idea how much longer we have on this earth. Only the very aged and terminally ill are unfortunate enough to have such information. As children, we assume we will live forever. High school seems a million years away. Eventually, we start remarking to one another how time flies by, and then it is "Oh my goodness Dorothy, can you believe another school year is over? Our children will be freshmen in the fall... Glory be!" I hear you chuckling, but you know what I am talking about!

Months and years will fly by and you may never get around to accomplishing the things you most want to do. If you have your key priorities in the front of your mind and work on them before anything else, things will automatically fall into place. Amazingly and without prioritizing them, laundry still gets done, bills are still paid, and social media still gets posted, liked, shared, retweeted, etc.

Our time bank is a finite account with an unknown balance that declines minute by minute and does not accept direct deposits. Sure, you can affect the balance by living a healthy life, driving carefully, and avoiding high-risk situations. However, once today is gone, it is lost forever. We must be careful not to procrastinate on the things we want to do while we have our youth and our health because one day it will be too late to do them at all.

"Remember being selfish is not the same as being self-indulgent. You have the gift of time. Use it to do what you love. Believe anything is possible and then work like hell to make it happen."

~ Julianna Margulies, American actress and producer

UNSTICKING MYSELF

Back to my earlier story … I was becoming increasingly restless in my killer job, and all of my family and friends could see it for what it was. On a whim over the holidays, I free typed my resume into a popular online job site. After a few weeks, I received a call from a company one zip code over from my hometown. We started the conversation that pivoted my career. The company had formed a brand new group, led by a VP from my alma mater. The work interested me and let me take a break from managing people for a while. Although they wrote the offer letter with different language, I interpreted it as, "work fewer hours for more money, without the travel, where you can buy your first home, reclaim your kitties from Mom and Dad, start dating for real again, take better care of yourself through cooking and exercise, and wear jeans to work daily." I politely inquired whether they preferred I sign in blood, or if ink would suffice.

Switching jobs and companies at that time was the best thing I could have done for my health and happiness. It was the absolute right move for me. I probably would be a more senior executive at my first corporation had I stuck with it, but the work and pace might have killed me by now. These things matter. I see my former colleagues who are still at that company higher up the corporate ladder than I am, yet I would not trade my life today for the world. Making that career shift then was part of the journey that led me to where I am now.

I do not deny that the experience I gained in the prior job has served me supremely. Experience is what it is, and you are the only one who can decide if that which you are accumulating is good or bad for you. I carved out a wonderful space for myself professionally while reconnecting with family and old high school friends, the most precious of whom I married several years later. A key lesson here is that there are many, many ways to find happiness, and just because you leave one "great opportunity" does not mean that you will never find the path to fulfillment. Who knows? Turning down that opportunity could be the decision needed to place you on the right track. Do not waste your precious time. Instead, spend it as if your life depends on it. It does.

I cannot emphasize enough how much time matters. While you can buy other people's time to some extent, your own is a use-it-or-lose-it resource. Consider the classic fable about a New York Wall Street businessman who takes a brief power-vacation to a remote Central American coastal village. After observing a local fisherman depart early in the morning to return a couple hours later. Seeing a boat just half full of fish, he chided the man.

"Why are you back so early with only half a boatload?" the businessman asked.

"I have caught all the fish I need to feed my family and my village for today. Now I am going to take a siesta, make love with my wife, and spend the afternoon playing with my children."

"Baah," the businessman said. "You should spend more time fishing. Take advantage of the whole day. Fill your whole boat with fish, maximize its capacity! Then, you can sell fish to the neighboring villages too."

"Why would I want to do that?" The fisherman was perplexed.

"So you can earn more money, buy a bigger boat, catch more fish, earn more money, and retire in ten or twenty years," the businessman exclaimed!

"And then what would I do?"

"You could enjoy an afternoon siesta, make love with your wife, and play with your children!"

"But señor, my children will be grown by then."

While funny, I also find this sad. We can always generate more money, but we can never create more time. There is the further question of when is enough, enough? While this answer differs for each individual, I highly recommend that we periodically ask the question of ourselves. You find yourself marooned on *Someday Isle*, waiting for when the time will be right to start following your dreams. Do you really need to wait, or can you find a way to integrate pursuing your dreams into your life today, while fulfilling your obligations?

Step one is making the decision to take action today instead of putting it off on tomorrow. Later, we will address proven strategies for doing this within the context of all the other very real obligations you have.

"And you are young, and life is long, and there is time to kill today.
And then one day you find - ten years have gone behind you.
No one told you when to run; you missed the starting gun..."

- Pink Floyd, "Time", The Dark Side of the Moon, Harvest Records, 1973

PART 1: DESTINATION ACTION CHALLENGES

Dream Your Own Dreams:

1. Reflect on the activities and experiences that bring you satisfaction long after the activity is over.
2. Answer for yourself the incredibly simple, incredibly tough question: "What do you sincerely want?" If you have no idea, create time and space to ponder this deeply.
3. Pause to do a quick dream self-assessment. Are these truly YOUR dreams and not someone else's?

Identify Your Why:

1. List in order of importance what you value most. Reference the table on page 27 for ideas.
2. Without biasing them, ask a few people to do the same activity on your behalf (top five is enough). See how your actions speak for themselves.
3. Scrutinize the differences between your self-assessment and those from others. Observe where your actions diverge from what you want your values to be.
4. Where you see mismatches, adjust your value statement or adjust your behaviors. If you are happy with life, simply face reality and accept your values for what they are.

Mission Statements:

1. Consider top three values you identified above. What does winning look like to you for each dimension?
   a. What will give you immense personal satisfaction?
   b. What does your life's work entail, and how can you magnify its impact?
   c. Will you choose to leave a legacy of some kind, and if so, what could it be?

42

2. Without putting any reality checks in place, articulate what you believe will make you the most fulfilled YOU possible.
   a. Start with your WHAT and your WHY.
      Set aside the HOW for now.
   b. Have faith that if you can dream it, you can create it.

Bucket List:

1. Start jotting down all the things you want to do, see, learn, and experience with your one precious life.
   a. Capture each idea at the level of detail you need to spark your excitement.
   b. Include at least a couple of big dreams that scare you at least a little.
2. After writing down everything you can imagine, organize them. Identify the ten that most excite you.
3. Add details:
   a. Who would you like to share these experiences with?
   b. Are they location dependent, and if so where?
   c. What prerequisites are implied within this list? Etc.
4. Select the one you want to bring to life first and start creating a plan to bring it to reality.
5. Elevate this Bucket List into a living, breathing, meaningful force in your life. Refresh it regularly.

Someday Isle:

1. What are you deferring to Someday Isle?
2. Decide on a goal you will take action on. Now turn to Part 2 with this goal in mind.

PART 2: (A) ATTITUDE

Attitude   noun at·ti·tude \ ˈa-tə-ˌtüd , -ˌtyüd \⁷

the way you think and feel about someone or something

a feeling or way of thinking that affects a person's behavior

Word Origin: First known use 1668

CHAPTER 4: A WINNING ATTITUDE

Dear Brooke,

I have this great idea, but I'm afraid it will never work. There are so many things that could go wrong, and I'm not sure it's worth the try. Sure, it could be amazing. It also could be a complete and total disaster. Everyone else seems to get the lucky break, but I'm just not good enough to make this come to fruition.

Calling All Wildly Successful Pessimists

<cue crickets chirping>

A large degree of life's success is driven by the attitude you bring to the party. Attitude can originate from what you learned, observed, or modeled in childhood, from those you surround yourself with today, or from within. You have the power to make a conscious decision about how you wish to approach this game called life. Given that attitude is not a predetermined part of your DNA, you hold the power to decide which lenses you use to view the world each day. I strongly believe choosing the can-do attitudes of optimism, resilience, gratitude, perseverance, and flexibility will serve you well. These are the currents which help you down the river of life.

I think you will be hard-pressed to come up with a robust list of wildly successful pessimists. I would argue that if they are doing well, it is both in spite of themselves and not to the highest level possible. How successful you become is largely determined by how successful you **expect yourself** to become. Unfortunately, pessimists usually expect the worst.

My younger daughter is the happiest person I know. It does not matter what is happening around her. She is always laughing and giggling, finding a reason to smile, including when she is in trouble. She constantly tries to make the rest of us laugh so we can all laugh along with her. Oh boy, does she have boundless energy! Our Wee One, at five years old, looks at the world with the most amazing bright eyes. When she wakes up, today is the best day ever. She laughs, she plays, and she loves life no matter what. She knows no other way. I hope she embraces that mindset forever.

Attitude is not everything, but it sure is powerful. The attitude we take affects our own likelihood for success and happiness, and it rubs off on those around us. I will never forget TSA Steve and the impact he had on me in the briefest of interactions.

Steve was the TSA inspector who greeted me in the Seattle-Tacoma International Airport one fine Sunday morning a few Aprils ago. I was starting my long journey home from Grama and GrampO's house. In his late forties, Steve sported a grey mustache and a warm smile that crinkled his eyes. His efforts often were unappreciated. On this particular morning, he was comparing identification cards to boarding passes at the A-N-S gates, helping shuttle travelers through the security procedures.

Upon reaching the front of the queue, I gave him my usual cheerful, "Hi! How are you?" My TSA goal is to be friendly and polite, but not extreme enough to trigger extended body cavity searches, and miss my flight. My general rule is not to expect much out of this mundane greeting, but this time proved to be a little bit different.

Rather than the normal, bored, sighed "fine" I expected in response, Steve replied, "I'm Excellent!" He paused, then continued, "But I'm trying to get better." He handed me my documents back and wished me a great day.

As I moved forward to the metal detectors, his words registered with me. I felt a grin cover my face when I registered what he had uttered. I turned back to say something, but he was already engaged with another traveler. I took note of his name and general appearance, then moved on my way.

His words have stuck with me, I confess I have stolen and recycled his response for myself. It tends to generate the same response I had: a few moments after you say it, the thought registers, and people start to chuckle. Nothing wrong with that.

Think about his attitude though!

I consider "how are you" to be a greeting and not an inquiry about one's health. Other than your closest friends and family, most people prefer not to hear about your aches and pains, or how tired you are, or how pissed off you are at the guy who cut you off, or whatever.

Sometimes your friends and family do not want to hear it either. Generally, they are expecting, "Fine, and you?" and that is the extent of it. When someone does say something other than "Fine...," nine times out of ten they are about to tell you something negative. What a surprise when Steve said he was excellent!

Secondly, I *love* the concept of being in a great place, and still trying to get better. The spirit of continuous improvement is a

wonderful thing, and for Steve, being "Excellent" was his starting point. In this example, excellent was not good enough for Steve and he was doing something about it. It cost him no time since his job had him standing there anyway. It fed rather than consumed energy from his spirit.

"I'm Excellent! But I'm trying to get better."

~ TSA Steve

WINNER WINNER, CHICKEN DINNER

We affect our environment, and our environment affects us. It has been said that we are the average of the five people we spend the most time with. If so, then we need to make sure we fill our lives and surround ourselves with winners. Winners can excel in any aspect of life - personal, professional, spiritual, athletic, creative, financial, you name it.

What are the key behavioral differences between the winners and losers in life? It starts with attitude, which behaviors reinforce. Here are some clues on the next page.

Winners 👍👎 Losers	
Believe they can. Obsess on figuring out how something can be done. Keep trying until they succeed with tenacity and persistence. Believe that impossible is merely an opinion.	Believe they cannot. Obsess around why something cannot be done. Give up at the first point of resistance or when things get hard. Believe that impossible is forever.
Take responsibility for their actions and the results thereof. Own and learn from their mistakes.	Blame everyone and everything, but themselves for their situation. Defend, justify, or deny their mistakes.
Focus on the positive with an attitude of gratitude. Celebrate wins large and small.	Complain about the hurdles, roadblocks, and losses. Downplay interim wins.
Choose short-term discomfort, inconvenience, pain, investment, and hard work for later gains.	Choose smaller immediate gratification over long-term investment gains.
Protect their resources and apply their time, talents, and money toward achieving their dreams.	Squander their assets and complain they never get what they want out of life.
Respect others and enrich their lives. Give, give, give. Build up others.	Take, take, take - tear down others, and complain when nobody wants to give them more. Demand entitlements.
Surround themselves with the positive energy of other winners. Passion and success love company.	Surround themselves with others who empower their mindset and complaining. Misery loves company.

Winners inspire those around them to be more, do more, think more, and achieve more. By their own example and their willingness to help others around them, they make the world better by living their life to the fullest and encouraging others to do the same. Winners are thinkers and doers who continuously focus on personal improvement and goal achievement. They are compulsive optimists and chronic problem solvers. Winners work hard and play hard. They do interesting things with interesting people. They take calculated risks, with an eye toward winning the game, rather than avoiding a loss. Winners manage their resources fiercely and reserve them for whatever they deem worthy. Lastly, they surround themselves with other winners, to parlay the magical energy of winning into greater successes and impact.

When you fill your life, time, and attention with winners, you crowd out the losers by default. You will have no time for them. You will force out the naysayers, the pessimists, and all the other Debbie Downers who promote the notion that misery loves company. I choose not to waste my precious time or energy with misery.

Given you have read this far, I know you do not either. So, in addition to those closest to you, how can you find others who will support or join you on your journey to excellence? Your network, of course. Surround yourself with the best, learn from the best, and in time, you will learn to be the best. At that point, you will seek out more winners who are playing in the next league up. If you are always the superlative amongst everyone you hang out with, you are hanging out with the wrong crowd. Nobody will push you to up your game, and you will miss out on the opportunity to learn from others. You need to find a bigger pond to swim around.

"I've missed more than 9000 shots in my career. I've lost almost 300 games. 26 times, I've been trusted to take the game-winning shot and missed. I've failed over and over and over again in my life. And that is why I succeed."

~ Michael Jordan, "the greatest basketball player of all time"[8]

GO BIG OR GO BIGGER

One of my favorite rules is the 10x rule. It forces me to think bigger and to be bolder because large problems do not get solved by thinking incrementally. If I want to retire one year early, I can probably pinch enough pennies to achieve this goal. If I want to retire ten years early, it takes a different mindset, and a different solution set. Pinching pennies may or may not get me there, but if they do, it will likely be a miserable existence. If I want to retire and live like the queen I wish to be, I need different ways to fund my retirement than scrimping and saving.

I saw this in action in the business world many years ago. The company where I worked was in a world of hurt. Its core technology (dial-up Internet) was rapidly being replaced by broadband. Compounding this, broadband itself was rapidly becoming a commodity. We had to devise massive spending reductions, while still improving our JD Power customer service scores and retaining the employees critical to keeping the business running.

We set up a program to *"Build a Better Businessperson"* as a proxy for a mini-MBA. We could not pay to send anyone to school, but we carved out time in everyone's week to teach anyone who was interested core lessons in marketing, finance, operations, etc. The capstone project was for each of the six working teams to find forty million dollars in net income for the next year, self-funding it in the process.

Our savings goal required only $4,000,000. Instead, we challenged each team to find us $40,000,000. If we had set the challenge to be to go find $4,000,000, we would have ended up with a list of small projects designed to find $100,000 here, $200,000 there. These small projects would have competed with one another for resources, and ultimately half would come to fruition. By asking for 10x more, we were hoping to stimulate bigger thinking.

The result was stunning. The teams were SO creative and resourceful, and blew everyone away. Every team not only found $40,000,000 of opportunity, between the revenue and cost sides of the equation, but in many situations, they found DIFFERENT opportunities. When we added all of the ideas from each team and removed duplicates, the collective group had over $200,000,000 worth of pretty great ideas. Some were definitely better and more feasible than others, but this contest solved the original problem with room to spare. It was illuminating. Remember, we only needed $4,000,000.

When you have a goal to attack, how would you have to think differently to achieve it in a significantly bigger way? If you had to come up with $10,000 instead of $1,000, what ideas would you consider? If you wanted to bicycle a hundred miles instead of ten, how might you approach training? If you wanted to publish ten books instead of one or sell a million copies instead of several thousand, what marketing strategies would you consider? Think boldly. Scaling back is generally easier than pushing bigger.

One blocker that seem to paralyze us from taking that 10x bigger path is the fear of failure. How you view problems makes a difference in how long they remain challenges. Kevin shared with me his winning strategy for handling the problems he runs into. His natural inclination had been to get angry when problems arose, which not only wasted his energy and put him into a negative frame of mind, but also solved nothing.

Now he reframes every problem he encounters into a goal to be achieved. It goes into the hopper to be prioritized according to its importance and urgency, then gets tackled along with everything else important in his life. He puts a plan in place, musters up the necessary resources to achieve it, and starts applying his energy toward it where needed. Kevin shared that while these goals may not be particularly exciting or energizing compared to some of his others, they help him keep a positive attitude while he knocks them out.

How can you simultaneously turn your problems *down* by a factor of ten while turning your goals *up* by that same factor? You can do it once you start putting your mind to it. Think big. Take full ownership, and be tenacious in working through your roadblocks.

"Sometimes it's harder not to be bold."

~Yana Lemann, friend

IN THE BLAME GAME, EVERYONE LOSES

Part of setting yourself up for success entails letting go of the incessant need to blame external forces for causing unhappiness, inconvenience, and inequities in our lives. Life is not fair.

Nobody said it would be fair.

Get over it.

With the exception of TSA Steve, I have had my share of frustrating travel experiences. With an unusual ferocity of summer thunderstorms, one flight I took from New York to Washington, DC came within twenty minutes of landing. It then was turned around to go all the way back to New York, presumably to get more gas. Upon arrival, we were told the flight was canceled, and all passengers were booked on the next available flight. As luck would have it, the airline rebooked me on the 6:00AM flight the following day. I was incredibly frustrated with this outcome.

I wanted to get mad at someone, to have someone apologize and take responsibility for my inconvenience, and to make everything right again. The problem is, there is no one to blame, and no amount of compensation could replace the time that I lost.

Nobody controls the weather. It follows its own whims. All the other surrounding airports were filled with planes that were diverted ahead of us. The gas tank is only so big, and so far nobody can magically make a commercial flight refill in the air.

Putting everything in perspective, the last time my flight turned around in the air and returned to its origin was at the beginning of a twenty-four hour journey home from the Philippines. That time, an unfortunate soul had a heart attack aboard our 747 and desperately needed urgent medical attention. He did not make it home. How could one fault that poor passenger under those circumstances? The New York flight paled by comparison.

What to do? I struggled to keep my peace and harmony on the inside, and somehow I succeeded. I had no control over the flight, yet I was determined to sleep in my own bed that night. I took the AirTrain to the Subway to Penn Station and bought a ticket on the next Amtrak train to Union Station in Washington, DC.

From there, I took the Metro to the end of the Orange Line, had my dearest one pick me up at the station, drive me thirty miles to my car at Dulles Airport, and I drove home from there. Planes, trains, and automobiles, and then some. On the upside, I also got to read two terrific books, one I brought with me, and one I picked up in Penn Station. I seldom make time to read for fun, so that was a bonus.

It is human nature to assign blame when we feel we have been wronged. Many seem to *need* someone to take the fall - that is to own up and pay for the transgression. It is fair to say we like to sue one another somewhat freely in America. You see questionable lawsuits and sometimes outrageous settlements.

Reality check: In many situations, *there is no one to blame*. Life happens. Rather than finding a way to get out of the bad situation quickly, many of us prefer to wallow in it while assigning blame instead. Energy goes into figuring out a way to profit from it instead of solving the original problem.

It is healthier to assess the existing situation, and decide what is the desired outcome. Examples might include:

"I want to get home tonight," or

"I will find a hotel and go see a Broadway show."

I recommend heartily against:

"I want the airlines to pay me lots of money for my inconvenience that they had nothing to do with, since they cannot control the weather either."

Put your energies instead toward reaching your desired outcome as smoothly as possible.

Secondly, as imperfect humans, we are uncomfortable being wrong. When something is going poorly in our lives, or if we underperformed on something, we seek a reason to explain it away.

- If I work too much, it is because the company made me.

  [I chose not to look for another job or talk to my boss about getting help.]

- If I am overweight, it is because the fast food companies do too good a job at marketing.

  [I chose not to make healthier food choices, or exercised too little.]

- If I lost my job, it is because my boss hates me.

  [I performed poorly, or my let skill sets became obsolete.]

As a general observation, blame is weak. It is a cop out. It is harder to take accountability for your own destiny, but you sure do go further in life. Taking responsibility and avoiding the blame game is one key difference between the winners and losers in life.

Do not blame. Do not blame me, do not blame yourself, do not blame God, the weather, or the President of the United States of America.

Take responsibility and ownership for what you should, and just let the rest go. Understand that so many bad events are nobody's fault. It is what it is. Even if someone did do something "against" you, what is done is done. It is now a fact of history. How you respond, and what you do next remains in YOUR hands. Blaming the catalyst only holds you back. Focus not on attributing blame to something that happened in the past, but rather shaping how your future is going to adapt to it. You must be resilient and deal with the present, with an eye toward improving the future.

There is a more powerful lesson to be captured here, once we acknowledge that blame is futile. We have the power to decide how to adapt to the circumstances we find ourselves in. Yes, bad things happen. Sometimes they happen to the best or most innocent of people. Letting yourself get spun up about the unfairness is a choice. You can swirl on it, or you can acknowledge and accept the situation and devote your energies to moving to a better place. Nobody said life would always be sunshine and roses. Floods and poison ivy happen too. Your call on how you choose to react.

"If you make it a habit not to blame others you will feel the growth of the ability to love in your soul, and you will see the growth of goodness in your life."

~ Count Lyov (Leo) Tolstoy, Russian author

CHAPTER 5: FEAR AND DOUBT

Dear Brooke,

I am afraid of stepping off the corporate ladder - what if I can't get back on? Worse yet, what if I take this leap and end up failing? I haven't the skills to do what I think I'd love and I definitely don't want to start all over at the bottom. I'm too old to be a newbie again. I neither want to risk my progress nor go backwards. I'm trapped by my own success, financially and hierarchically. Go figure. I'm too successful to be happy.

WHAT'S THE WORST THAT CAN HAPPEN?

I wrote earlier about the 10x rule. It sounds great to say, "Hey, rather than doing something, do it an order of magnitude larger." Keeping it real, I recognize that getting started on the first goal is daunting enough, let alone a 10x goal. Two things often hold me back: (1) fear, and (2) not knowing how to get started.

We will address getting started in Part 4, but let's address fear now. It occupies the imagination more often than reality. Fear has been described as the *anticipation* of pain, rather than the actual pain itself. It has not yet happened, but we feel the anxiety and discomfort anyway.[9]

Sometimes the problem is the premonition of future failure. I appreciate the catchphrase that fear simply stands for: False Evidence Appearing Real. Whether real or not, if in our minds the saber-toothed tiger stalks us, we need to deal with it before it causes us harm. Ask yourself whether the fear actually threatens your own health and well-being, or more accurately intimidates your comfort zone.

I vividly remember the weekend I spent in Boulder, Colorado. I booked a flight from Milwaukee to Denver on a Friday afternoon in late August. Sunbeams shone through the airport terminal windows as the sun sank toward the horizon, while I waited for the inbound plane to arrive. Vacationers departing for quick getaways jostled with business travelers returning home for the weekend. The details are so clear to me eighteen years later.

My solo trip's purpose was that of an advance scout for the team I was joining two weeks later. I had come off a rough assignment after struggling to figure out the new job I had taken. This was the start of my second gig and I felt completely in over my head. While on the surface none of the work was difficult, I perceived great risk if I were to mess up my tasks. A blazing headache started on the plane that Friday evening, and it persisted throughout the entire weekend. I could not shake my overwhelming feeling of anxiety.

I was in one of the most beautiful parts of the United States, a crunchy granola type of town nestled into the Rocky Mountains. My hotel was comfortable and within an easy walking distance to the town center where great restaurants and shops welcomed travelers and locals alike. I took a walk in the foothills so that I could exercise my body and try to clear my mind. I was oblivious to the beauty surrounding me. I was trapped in my head worrying, though I could not articulate why I was so incredibly stressed out.

Sunday evening, I found myself sitting alone in a sports bar for a bite of dinner. Though a dozen TVs displayed highlights from preseason football, I paid them little attention. The server took my order then left me to my thoughts. A voice inside my head asked:

What's the worst that can happen?

Um, excuse me? Who's in there?? It was a strange and unprecedented experience for me.

"What's the worst that can happen?"

When the server passed by again, I asked for a pen and a scrap of paper, which he kindly provided.

I then started listing all the possible things that could go wrong, followed by the consequences, both probable and worst case scenarios. Interestingly, none of the potential outcomes resulted in death or dismemberment. If I stretched my imagination, I *possibly* could have lost my job, but when I looked at it objectively in writing, highly unlikely. The worst realistic possible outcome is that I would have either annoyed or disappointed my new team or possibly slowed them down by a few days. All things considered, not a big deal. It was FEAR - false evidence appearing real. It was my comfort zone being threatened by doing something new, but never threatening to my life or limb.

The tension dissolved from my shoulders, and my headache vanished faster than I ever would have expected. The server brought my cheeseburger. While eating, I noticed the sunset starting to crescendo over the foothills outside the window. The magnificence took my breath away. I took an after-dinner walk and finally noticed what a beautiful place I was in. It had completely gone unnoticed before. My regret was not having done this simple and quick risk assessment sooner, so I could have moved past it and enjoyed my time in Boulder. I did go on and make the most of my last twenty-four hours in town, but the most memorable experience was feeling this tension physically drain out of my body. I have thought back on this moment dozens of times throughout my life, and the ability to do the "what's the worst that can happen" exercise was Boulder's gift to me.

Since that Sunday afternoon, I have heard others share similar stories. Some take this a step further to identify what they can do to prevent the bad outcome, or to develop their game plan for fixing the mess when it cannot be prevented. Sometimes effective preventative measures are surprisingly easy to put in place. Other times you may find it is not worth the cost or effort to prevent the unlikely bad outcome from happening; the repair afterwards may not be too bad. Just the exercise alone of thinking through the possible outcomes can ease your fears and spur you to action.

Little in life is irreversible, with the exceptions of (1) bringing a life into or taking a life out of this world and (2) the passage of time. Look your fear in the eyes and objectively assess the actual likelihood of pain. Is it real or more of a vague unknown? Take a risk, enjoy coloring outside the lines. And if you do something stupid ... do not get caught.

"I've had a lot of worries in my life, most of which never happened."

~ Mark Twain, American Author

INNATE COURAGE

In this vein, we can learn a lot from the youngest of our society. Children are born wanting to learn and to succeed. There is a fearlessness helping them try scary skills they have never attempted. Think about how many children would ever learn to walk if there was an intuitive fear of falling or failure. Adults instill this fear.

In many ways fear is a powerful survival skill. Keeping their children from falling off tall objects or out of a window is a parental duty. Sometimes I wonder if we go too far though, where some families' children are so completely protected from ever experiencing failure as a child that they never learn how to manage through it once they become older. They are so afraid of falling that they never attempt to leap. It is a challenge for parents to know where to draw that line - allowing enough failure for children to learn how to work through it while protecting them from legitimately hurting themselves.

By adulthood, we are programmed to respond to the conditioning our early years gave us. We have habits, beliefs, and attitudes that help us live the exact life we are currently experiencing. If we love our life, then these thought patterns are supporting us in winning. If we want our lives to be different, the good news is that this is software coding, not hard wiring. We will have to overcome habits, and while not easy, the brain is elastic and reprogrammable throughout the duration of each life.

I started educating myself on how machine learning is changing the world from customized Netflix recommendations to Facebook facial recognition to Tesla's self-driving cars. What struck me is how algorithms learn best by learning like a child. Computers are fed a ton of unstructured data - documents, images, numbers, sounds, characters, etc. - and allowed to figure it out.

This is no different from how a child learns. Children are never given an instruction manual at birth to teach them first to crawl, then walk, then run. They observe the world around them and put themselves out there. They experiment, practice, fail and succeed. In the earliest of days, the concept of embarrassment or fear of failing on the public stage is hardly a consideration. It's all about "Look at me!" and "Watch what I can do!" and "Let ME try!" There is an innate courage the luckiest of us never lose. Too often the majority of us surrender early on.

How do we overcome this? It is through making the decision to be bold. To power through fear. To be afraid and to do it anyway.

We have to steer into the wind sometimes to get to where we want to go. As any sailor knows, you cannot go only the way the wind is blowing, or you may never make it back to your home port. You need to learn how to point your bow into the wind, then tack your sail, traveling in a zigzag pattern so the wind will still take you wherever your heart desires as it shifts from one side of your boat to the other. You steer into the wind, and while it may not be as easy, you maintain control of your destination. Where there is a will, there is always a way.

Muster your courage and control your attitude and the world can be yours. How you push your comfort zone will influence your resilience and outlook.

"Courage doesn't necessarily mean the absence of fear."

~Doyle Brunson, Two-time World Series of Poker Main Event champion

LESSONS FROM ELMO

I confess I consider Elmo to be a pretty good role model, particularly when it comes to attitude. As parents of young children, we slowly let TV into their lives. When she was a baby, our oldest mostly watched Sunday football games and Sports Center with an occasional hockey game thrown in for balance.

Once Baby Girl became cognizant of the TV (and when I needed a distraction for her while feeding her brother), we started venturing into Baby Einstein. At first, this seemed like a boring, trippy, experience. How on earth are they making money from low-budget videos of toys and ordinary kids? We quickly recognized it to be baby crack, which also had a calming effect on us adults too. It was absolutely fascinating.

After watching every Baby Einstein episode a million times, the next evolutionary TV step was Sesame Street. I remember it from my childhood as colorful Muppets and friendly, goofy adults sponsored each week by two letters and a number.

Now I have not been living so deeply under rocks to be totally oblivious to Elmo. I recall when the Tickle Me Elmo stampedes were in the news. I figured this was an updated version of the Cabbage Patch riots of 1983.[10] My take on Elmo was: very red, very annoying, and for some unknown reason, very beloved by children everywhere. For our own sanity, we were not inviting Elmo into our home unnecessarily.

This is where modern-day Sesame Street came into play. While feeding the baby, I put it on TV. My conclusions are:

1. The adults are still both friendly and goofy. They sing a lot. Their songs (and the earnestness with which they sing them) crack me up, which speaks to point #2.

2. The Sesame Street writers are *hysterical*. They are writing for the kids, but they slip in some zingers for the adults too.

Elmo, dare I say it, is a fabulous role model. I do not care for Elmo's World, but I love his daily interactions on Sesame Street with the other Muppets and the friendly, goofy adults. It took me a few episodes to come to this conclusion.

If you can get past his high-pitched, annoying voice, he is unfailingly positive.

If he cannot get what he wants immediately, he waits patiently.

If he never gets what he wants, he pretends.

He is friendly and kind to everyone he interacts with, and never has a bad word to say about anyone.

He is curious, and he is willing to try new things.

He smiles, he laughs, and he loves.

His attitude is so powerful. How on earth can a child NOT fall in love with this red fur ball? Kudos, Elmo! You have another fan.

We are never too old to open our minds to new ideas and new influences. The more we can see the world through our children's eyes, the younger we stay.

Elmo, I am watching you. Do not let me down, and never grow up! Keep looking at the world through optimistic, smiling eyes. The children - and some of us grown-up kids - are watching you.

Given that our brains and bodies respond to the thoughts we feed it, our attitude and self-beliefs are strong predictors of our ultimate results. Those who, like Elmo, expect that they will figure out how to solve the problems they encounter are the ones who do. Those who expect to be derailed by distractions or detractors usually are. Those who expect to win generally find a way to win, and those who expect to lose almost always do.

It all starts with the stories in our heads, which means the key to changing the ending resides within each of us. Will your life be a Drama? Romance? Comedy? Tragedy? Morality Play? Your screenplay is largely up to you and the stories you create and reinforce for yourself. You are its writer and you hold the pen.

"Ha ha ha, Elmo loves you!"

~ Elmo, furry red monster

SAME PLANET, DIFFERENT WORLDS

One of the best ways to try new experiences and push your comfort zone is through travel. The world is full of strange and different customs with unlimited ways to live a full and happy (or empty and terrible) life. Yours is neither the best nor the only way to go.

I wish everyone would take the time and the risk to go experience another culture, language, and way of life. Better yet, I wish everyone would do this before the age of twelve. Old enough to remember and experience; young enough to have an open mind about it.

I have to give mad props to Miss Jay. Jay arrived in late July 2016 from Brazil to spend a year with Team Lennon. She came to be our resident au pair. It scared us to invite an almost stranger into our home and entrust our three most prized possessions to her.

Despite being self-conscious of her English and being a stranger in a strange land, she left her friends, family, and devoted boyfriend to take a chance. I cannot begin to imagine how it felt to Jay, flying several thousand miles away from home to the top half of the world without knowing anybody. She took a risk to pursue her dream of spending time in the United States.

Twenty years younger than I, she has a lot more courage at that age than I did. Unknowingly, she encouraged me each day to face my fears, take a chance, and do things even when I knew I would not always do them flawlessly on my first try. Unsure of what the day would bring, she put on a brave game face and emerged from her room with a smile. Strange foods, strange routines, strange people, strange words. Smile smile, smile, smile. She took a chance on us, boarded a plane, and experienced rapid personal growth over the course of a year.

I traveled extensively with my job when I was younger. I had the advantages of having companies paying the bills, traveling with other colleagues, and being in English-speaking offices in almost all situations. Regardless of taking the first-class route, I still know the experiences I gained by venturing out into the world shaped who I am. The safest place for a ship is the harbor, but ships were never meant to live in harbors. Neither are we.

One of the most useful lessons I learned in my travels was creative communication. The most remote location where I spent significant time was Tomioka, Japan. Tomioka is a small fishing village a few miles south of the Fukushima Nuclear Power Plants. This is the one that suffered a level 7 nuclear meltdown, following the tsunami after the 9.0 magnitude earthquake on March 11, 2011.

I was there on several visits in the late 1990s, doing routine maintenance work. As a 5'7" "blonde" (not really, but blonde is relative), white American girl, I stood out like a sore thumb. The whole town knew of my presence, why I was there, and more than a few strangers knew my name despite the other hundred *gaijin* (foreigners) on site at the time. It was surreal.

We lived in the town, sometimes in the business travelers' hotel, other times in rented flats. I experienced the power of both Charades and Pictionary to communicate with gestures and drawings. I learned that a smile goes a long way, as do patience and willingness to persevere.

Learning basic words in the local language is both prudent and courteous. I recommend hello, goodbye, yes, no, please, thank you, "this is delicious," "how much does this cost?" "one cold beer please," and "where is the restroom?" to be a great starting set for your vocabulary. At one point I had these words and phrases down in at least ten different languages. "How do I start the Jacuzzi jets in the public baths?" turned out to be more challenging. I never did learn how to turn the bubbles on by myself.

The rule of thumb is that the words you use account for a mere seven (7) percent of comprehension. Fifty-five (55) percent of communication is in what your body language conveys, and the remaining thirty-eight (38) percent is in how you say it, including tone of voice, speed, pitch, etc.

You do not need to know the words being said to understand when someone is angry, excited, delighted, concerned, grief-stricken, contemptuous, or bored. The emotion lives all over your face and posture. You feel it viscerally through how they speak their incomprehensible words. So, while traveling or interacting cross-culturally, choose your words wisely. Choose your face and your tone with extreme care.

I share this because travel provides such an opportunity for rapid learning and comfort zone expansion. Your eyes are opened much wider by trying to communicate in a way that allows you to meet your daily needs. The difference in Miss Jay's English skills between the day she arrived and when we returned her to the airport fifty-one weeks later was astounding. Improvements notwithstanding, she still WAS able to communicate on day one; it just was not through relying solely on her English skills or Google Translate.

You learn to be flexible and resilient. You try new foods. You discover new sleeping configurations, and you learn that nothing is universally consistent. You may even learn new ways to use the restroom. For example, the commodes in Japan ranged from holes in the ground (two steps down from the typical squatty potties) to veritable Cadillacs, with a soft, padded, heated toilet seat, complete with remote control, built-in bidet, music, and white noise to cover your own noises. I urge you to go experience these kind of spectrums for yourself, with an open heart and open mind.

"Travel is the enemy of Prejudice."

~Anonymous MIT student I encountered in the career center, circa 1994

CHAPTER 6: IT'S ALL IN YOUR IMAGINATION

Dear Brooke,

What I want to be isn't who I am. I can't code, I'm not a techie. I'm not cut out to be a parent. I don't know the first thing about international travel. Who am I to write a book, I'm not an author! I'm too old of a Dog to learn new tricks - how can I possibly become a Wolf? I want to be a Wolf, but that's not part of the canine DNA I'm stuck with.

DON'T BELIEVE EVERYTHING YOU THINK

One of the greatest catalysts for growth is being open to new ideas and allowing yourself to change your mind. A common trap almost everyone falls into is the *Confirmation Bias*. This is the tendency to interpret new evidence as confirmation of one's preexisting beliefs, hypotheses, or theories. Nobody wants to be wrong; hence, we naturally try to continually prove to ourselves (and everyone else) how right we are. This cripples our growth potential, and frankly, our relationship potential too. I have learned the most powerful way to end an argument is by saying three little magic words, "I was wrong." Who will argue with you over that?

While young, we tend to make declarations of life as either black or white. My dad often recounts his story of earning his undergraduate business degree and earning consistent Bs and Cs. He regularly submitted black or white answers to his case studies leaving little room for the subtle nuances of the human condition. Four years later when he returned for his MBA, he aced his classes when he saw and presented all the shades of grey in-between. Same business curriculum - different way of looking at life.

I now believe that life is neither black and white nor the clichéd shades of grey. It implies excess linearity in an extremely non-linear universe. I like to think that everything between black and white is a vast continual spectrum of all colors of the rainbow, with variations in hue, intensity, and saturation to boot.

In the Crayola™ universe, white is the absence, and black is the presence of all colors. A rainbow in-between only makes sense. Then again, in light, it is exactly the opposite as evidenced by the prisms that split white light into the spectrum and the black holes containing effectively nothing. Such a simple illustration of this shows that if we cannot agree on what is black and what is white, how on earth can we agree upon anything between the two? Furthermore, we are likely to change our own minds on what seems like such simple questions: what is black, what is white? Give yourself permission to examine your beliefs and change your mind at any time.

While tidying up my office, I flipped through and retired old notebooks. Some dated back over ten years and five business models ago. I came across a quotation of note from my old buddy Benjamin, who in the summer of 2004 remarked, "At some point, I'd like to eat every part of a pig."

It made me laugh as much today as on the day he said it. It prompted me to drop a quick note to the old team to say hi and share my giggle. Benjamin messaged me back shortly thereafter, with the wise observations, "Amazin' quote ... genius. Don't know if I still hold to that belief!" I chuckled and suggested to him, "Don't believe everything you think. Down the line, you may find you disagree with your younger self."

Ouch, right? Today, each of us is pretty sure that whatever we believe is the truth (otherwise, by definition - we would not believe it), including those of us who know we do not know everything. We know our beliefs though, and gosh-darn-it, THEY ARE VALID {insert some adamant podium thumping here}.

OK! Slow down, Nelly. Logically, it is IMPOSSIBLE for us ALL to be right about EVERYTHING. Any two perfectly smart, educated, and rational people will have at least one fundamental thing they disagree on. Our beliefs are fluid, changing and evolving with each day that passes. We consider new ideas, experience cold-hard-reality, and gain a little wisdom. With each ride around the sun, we grow as individuals, gain perspective, and adjust our beliefs along the way.

The funny thing is the longer time goes on, as I told Benjamin, the greater the chances are that we now disagree with our younger selves. Project this forward. In another twenty years, you will be disagreeing with the YOU of today. It offers definite food for thought. Maybe some of your beliefs today may not stand the test of your own time and perspective, let alone everyone else's. Good grief, now we not only disagree with everyone else in the world, but we disagree with ourselves as well.

A lady I know through my network shared with me the story of how a single conversation changed her point of view a full 180 degrees. A family member is a fairly dedicated *prepper*. If you are not familiar with the term, it is someone who believes in the high likelihood of a catastrophic disaster, war, or other major emergency. Whether the crisis is natural or manmade, the philosophy is to be prepared for whatever comes your way.

Preppers are not one size fits all; some focus on stockpiling weapons and ammunition, building explosion-proof concrete bunkers, and stockpiling canned goods and potable water. Others focus more on creating sustainable agriculture and alternative energy sources, to be independent of the conventional food and electricity supplies. Most hone various survival skills and take the Boy Scout motto to its fullest manifestation. I personally know and respect several variations of preppers.

Mary was sitting on her Mama's porch talking with a relative, who is fully engaged in preparedness. It is a significant part of his life, and he often speaks to those around him on the topic. He had been after her to do something to protect her family. She was thoroughly unconvinced of its necessity and had brushed off the conversation, until this particular day. A single question pivoted her life.

What if you're wrong?

This one thought took her breath away. If she was right, nothing changed. But if she was wrong, she could be watching her three children starve. Her risk of being wrong disproportionately outweighed the risk of being right.

She began looking at food options and guns. She started her search for a farm. Today she has a couple hundred acres, with livestock, a creek, space to grow crops, and a bonus underground bunker with a colorful history of its own. Her children are all grown and out of the house, but her peace of mind remains at home. This all originated with one question, and the willingness to challenge her own thinking. She changed her mind in a heartbeat, and it changed her life.

Context matters. Next time you adamantly stand up on your soapbox, give pause. Be open-minded to hearing out the beliefs of others and challenging your own. Remember others believe as strongly in theirs as you do in yours, and who is to say who is right and who is wrong?

Examine your beliefs periodically. Brutally evaluate whether they are your beliefs from today, or unexamined leftovers from a younger you. It is common to return to where you began; you may find that this self-examination reinforces those beliefs stronger than ever. Equally copacetic is discarding an obsolete belief that no longer is a part of you, despite once defending it to the bitter end. Your own growth and evolution will progress with or without your consent. Go with the flow and do not take yourself too seriously along the way.

Not only do we benefit from allowing our minds to change, but moreover we have the power to change them on purpose. Assimilating new information changes the brain, and this capability is referred to as neuroplasticity. The brain reorganizes itself after birth, as the new child internalizes, organizes, and ingests information about the world. Neuroplasticity allows us to relearn new or alternate skills as compensates for brain injury. Lastly, the adult brain can continue developing and forming new connections with each new piece of information learned or memorized. We "rewire" our brains by creating new neural pathways as adults. We can leave this up to chance, or put deliberate inputs in, to direct what output we hope to drive. It is a form of magic that most people do not realize they possess.

Be open to NOT believing everything you think. Explore new ideas that may seem crazy, while also challenging your own deeply held truths. Occasionally I ask Husband if I am starting to sound like a cuckoo new age cat lady. He just smiles. Remember that Jules Verne seemed pretty out there when he wrote about living under the sea in 1870. Today we have an entire Navy nuclear submarine fleet.

In 1974, science fiction writer Arthur C. Clarke was interviewed on video by the Australian Broadcast Corporation predicting personal computers and the Internet of the future, where every home would connect to everything. Indirectly, he predicted online banking and Fandango in the same minute and a half interview. He observed,

"The big difference when [the young boy sitting nearby] grows up... the year 2001 is that he will have in his own house not a computer as big as this, but at least a console through which he can talk to his friendly local computer and get all the information he needs for his everyday life, like his bank statements, his theater reservations, all the information you need in the course of living in a complex society. This will be in a compact form in his own house. It will have a television screen like these here and a keyboard and he will talk to the computer and get information from it. And he will take it as much for granted as we take the telephone."

I am sure that sounded like crazy fantasy talk back then when nobody owned a personal computer of any variety, let alone the ability to manage their lives on one. While several science fiction writers dreamed up variations of this thing we now know as the Internet, only a visionary few internalized its implications in the days of Disco and Nixon. While the juvenile Internet had been around for only half a decade and email was celebrating its third birthday, only the Department of Defense and a few universities spent time thinking hard about it. Everybody else went about their business in analog. Almost nobody could predict the impacts of the Information Age on our day-to-day lives forty years ago. Who knows what forty years from now will bring? Surely we each will change our minds about something.

Think back on what you believed strongly ten years ago. Whether you were a teenager or a grandparent a decade ago, identify three beliefs you held then. Were you infatuated with somebody you never thought you could live your life without? I bet you remember their name, but how about the birth date of this soul mate of yours? Have your political views strengthened or mellowed out? Your take on religion perhaps? Identify a few core beliefs that you know evolved over time for the sole purpose of recognizing that you and your thinking have shifted before. Be assured they will evolve again in the future.

Consider your three deepest held beliefs today - ideas so obvious to you that they need no debate. Taking one at a time, what might a completely opposite construct look like? What might a slightly different version be? How could you make these alternate realities work? When you look out the window and notice the sky is blue and the leaves are green, is it conceivably possible that your next door neighbor, while calling them blue and green, to see what you know as red and purple? Might the rods and cones in their eyes work slightly different than yours? If beauty is in the eye of the beholder, maybe we see things differently but do not know it because nobody else can see through our own unique pupils.

Lastly, think about something you consider impossible. How do you know? What might reduce its impossibility?

"The man who views the world at fifty, the same as he did at twenty, has wasted thirty years of his life."

~Muhammad Ali, American professional boxer and activist

DON'T BELIEVE EVERYTHING EVERYONE ELSE THINKS EITHER

While it is important not to take your own thoughts and word as gospel, think independently and avoid automatically taking everyone else's word as gospel too. Conventional wisdom is not always wise, and doing something because that is always how it has been done stands in the way of innovation and progress.

I love the *Monkeys in a Cage* story because it epitomizes this phenomenon. Recently my colleague Patrick was shaking his head over some technical requirements another team provided. They boiled down to, "We want our future digital process to do exactly what our antiquated, sub-optimal, manual one does because that is just the way we do it." He was stunned nobody else recognized how limiting and artificially restrictive the policies and practices were, or considered how we could be doing things in a better, simpler way. It seemed like the right time to call in the monkeys.

I do not know whether this research is real or corporate urban legend, but the story starts with a researcher and half dozen monkeys. The researcher put the monkeys in a cage together with a large bunch of perfectly ripe bananas suspended from the ceiling. Directly below was a convenient step ladder. Not surprisingly, the monkeys noticed the bananas, saw the step ladder, and ascended to get their prize. Once a monkey passed the second rung, research assistants blasted all six monkeys with a fire hose until the climber got off the ladder. This continued day and night until no monkey dared attempt the climb.

Next, one of the conditioned monkeys was swapped out for a new monkey. Our new friend noticed the bananas, saw the step ladder, and stepped on the first rung. Immediately, the five remaining monkeys tore the new one off the ladder. This repeated until the new monkey no longer attempted to reach for his prize.

In sequence thereafter, this process repeated itself. A new monkey replaced one of the original six, attempted to climb the

ladder, and his peers tore him down until he gave up. This continued until the cage was occupied by six new monkeys and one untouched bunch of bananas. None of these six had ever been sprayed with the fire hose, but they knew from the behavior of their peers not to climb the ladder. The bananas were off limits.

Nobody knew why. They just knew the dealio. You do not climb the ladder, you do not score the bananas, and you have no idea why. Conventional wisdom often goes unchallenged. Until someone willing to go against it does, the bananas never get captured.

Think about experiences in your life that do not make sense. Is it possible that they are the result of old news that no longer is relevant? Can you challenge any conventional thinking that may be standing in your way? There may be a wonderful bunch of perfectly ripe bananas waiting for you on the other side.

"I trust the eyes of an honest man more than I trust what everybody knows."

~Tyrion Lannister, Game of Thrones, Season 7, Episode 3

VISUALIZATION

Recognizing that our beliefs are all in our head and that we can change them opens up a world of possibility. What if we can use this malleability to our advantage? We can. We can deliberately shape our beliefs to work for and help propel us to our destination.

Athletes use visualization to rehearse hitting their shots straight down the fairway, or sticking the perfect landing. Musicians use visualization to experience their solos with perfect pitch and rhythm. Public speakers visualize the audience responding to their presentations with exactly the right timing and delivery, prompting laughter, surprise, or outrage at just the right moments.

It is a powerful mind hack. The brain cannot distinguish between reality and vivid imagination, so put this quirk to good use. When you cannot physically experience something you dearly want, start vigorously imagining it. It feels awkward at first, but with practice, anybody can use this technique to improve almost any aspect of life.

Focus your thoughts each day on the positive outcomes you expect for your life. Visualize how success looks, feels, sounds, tastes, and smells. The more multisensory the visualization, the more effective and powerful it is. When you are living your wildly successful life, describe your reality. Is your family in a loving, functional, harmonious state? Are you performing in front of a large, rapt audience? Are you in a position of political power where you are influencing the direction of your community? Are you launching your new business, or a new product line, or selling your millionth copy of your best-selling book series? Are you traveling the world or building your off-the-grid self-sustaining prepper house? What do these things smell like?

When you sit down to eat, who is at the table with you? What is served? Is it a presidential dinner in the White House, or a fully organic vegan meal prepared by loving hands? What scents greet your nose? Are they the smells of the vibrant crazy city you have always wanted to live in, or the scents of the cologne your true love favors? Are you feeling white sand beaches between your bare toes or the soft fuzz of a newborn's head nestled under your chin?

Visualize what success is to you by using all your senses. Add an overlay of the satisfaction you will feel when it is accomplished and you are living it in the moment.

As I write this chapter, I can feel the gentle rocking of the cruise ship I boarded earlier today headed for the western Caribbean. While part of my heart is home with my children and their phenomenal caregivers, I am excited for when they will be old enough to travel with us and to experience the gift of seeing the world. Writing this book is a dream and a personal goal, and I am enjoying the opportunity to sit uninterrupted and share my thoughts in writing. Quiet music plays in the background and I hear the hum of happy vacationers passing by me. Scents of dinner around me are strengthening, and the window on my right has darkened with the sunset. Right here, right now, there is nowhere else I wish to be. I experience it with each of my senses and commit it to memory to draw upon another time.

What do your various happy places do to your senses? Can you conjure them up in great detail in your imagination? Can you sense the successes now to help align your energies to bring them to life? If you have not tried this, I recommend incorporating visualization into your daily routines, if only for five minutes at the beginning of the day. The mind is a curious thing in that it cannot distinguish between *real* and *vividly imagined*. The more you visualize in sharp detail that which you want, the more your brain gets accustomed to it and naturally self-corrects toward it. By intentionally putting positive "pre-memories" into it, your mind will remember that which you wish it to and gravitate your life toward that. You create déjà vu by imagining your future, then working to bring it to fruition.

Focus your thinking on what you want, and not what you do not want. The mind hones in on keywords and often ignores the negation (the "not"). For example, instead of saying you "do not want to be alone" where the brain latches onto the keyword "alone", tell yourself you "will find a loving, supportive friend [partner, spouse]". The brain will connect with the words loving, supportive, and friend/partner/spouse (depending on what you tell it).

There is a popularly held belief about the *Law of Attraction*. In short, the universe conspires to give you that which you think about and ask for the most. Part of this is because when you focus your thinking on a goal, you start to notice more readily applicable resources that surround you. An expert could emerge in an area that will help you create your attack plan. Maybe you identify like-minded people simply because you start the conversation about your passion-point, signaling others to chime in. Sometimes you connect the dots between your goal and something unrelated in a new and interesting way. Maybe cheerleaders emerge from the crowd, who cannot help directly with your achievement but can provide encouragement when you most need a boost. If you do not keep these dreams on the forefront of your mind - thinking, talking, and obsessing about them all the time - your extra resources may miss the signal to come out of the woodwork.

In addition to focusing on what you want, preoccupy yourself with your Cans instead of your Cannots. After your "I would love..." statement, do you follow it with a "but I could never because..." thought? Challenge yourself on that self-limiting belief. If you are unable to do something today, is it a life sentence? Can some classes or training or practice turn the cannot into a can? If not, who else could do it for you? Outsourcing is often an answer if doing something yourself sub-optimizes the quality or speed you need. If money is tight, can you find an opportunity to barter a skill you are excellent at for something you need? Where there is a will, there is a way, and you will find the way once you decide that it is worth it. Do not let YOU be the thing keeping you from that which you want the most in life.

Remember that there is no statute of limitations on starting over or reinventing yourself. Strip away the reasons why your wishes elude you and what is holding you back. Get laser focused on what the wish or the dream itself is. What do you want at a visceral level? Frame that up into a mission statement of what you want your future to hold. We will work on overcoming the speed bumps later to get you unstuck from the rocks in your own riverbed.

"Visualization is the human being's vehicle to the future - good, bad, or indifferent. It's strictly in our control."

~ Earl Nightingale, American radio speaker and author

TAKE A HEAD TRIP

Perhaps you are homebound right now and cannot leave your zip code, or worse, your home. Sometimes this cannot be avoided but it does not prevent you from taking action. Here are some ideas:

Explore new ideas, cultures, languages, and perspectives from the comfort of your armchair, teenage bedroom, or even a jail cell. Books, podcasts, TV programs, the internet, and those who live within walking distance are all potential sources of inspiration. Be open to talking with someone you normally would not seek out, or to listening to a random TED talk[11] vs. selecting the topic.

- Learn a new language in a classroom, online, or through immersion with foreign TV shows. I have several friends who were born overseas and immigrated to the US as children. They learned English by watching American cartoons on TV, with Tom and Jerry, Mighty Mouse, the Flintstones, and Scooby Doo as their teachers.

- Make a new friend from somewhere else and get to know him or her at the core. Our natural inclination is to seek out others who look, talk, and think just like us. Take a deliberate step out of your comfort zone and introduce yourself to the new person at work, school, or in the neighborhood. Collect bonus points if that person is quite different from yourself.

- If you cannot leave your zip code, reach out to someone who left theirs to come to you. Chances are that he or she is looking for a new friend too.

- If you cannot leave your home, engage with others online. The internet is making the world smaller - choose an online group focused on your favorite interest, and interact with others who share your interest but live half a world away. You already have a built-in topic to discuss.

- Regardless of where you are, read books written in other countries and languages (translated into your own).

Ann Morgan presented a wonderful TED talk on this topic. Ann is a Londoner who made it her personal mission to read a book written from every country in the course of a year[12]. This presented some interesting challenges, starting with defining what the actual list of countries on earth is. One would think this would be Googleable but with country lines redefined continually, the answer is fluid. She landed on a list of 196 based on the UN's definition at the time.

Next came finding books translated into English from each of these countries. For the vast majority of countries, not a problem. For the smaller and less cosmopolitan ones, nonexistent. Sometimes written stories in the local language do not exist. Incredibly, as her quest gained publicity people started sending her books from their countries that they loved. More stunningly, in countries where English transcriptions did not exist, people worked together to transcribe books for her.

When your feet cannot travel, your imagination and emotions can. I urge you to take a round trip journey in your mind. Engage your imagination and visualize a different reality. Try something new, explore different ways to think, and look at the world a few degrees differently every now and again.

"If we could sell our experiences for what they cost us, we'd all be millionaires"

- Pauline Phillips writing as "Dear Abby," advice columnist

CHAPTER 7: SHACKLES AND OBLIGATIONS

Dear Brooke,

I have very real obligations. I'm buried under a large mortgage, car payments, student loans, and credit card debt. I can't just quit my life to run off to the third world to live as a painter poet! My kids and my parents need me. I'm stuck in the sandwich generation, with no relief in sight while my own relationship struggles to survive all these pressures. Living my dreams sounds great and all, but at the moment I just need a good night's sleep, and fewer worries.

If You're Going Through Hell, Keep Going

We each have our own unique, custom-tailored version of hell and have visited there at one or more points in our lives. For some, hell is when life deals one crippling blow after another and forces thoughts on how to survive until the next day. For others, it may be a void – loneliness, boredom, lack of sense of purpose in life. It also may be severe illness, physical or mental disabilities, or societal disadvantage, prejudice, or persecution. Hell goes well beyond our classic images of Biblical fire and brimstone.

As previously mentioned, Dr. Frankl's research in Auschwitz and Dachau showed that those who have a purpose to keep on going, do. Those who give up hope and let their circumstances overpower their will to thrive, perish. All else being equal, physical health coming into the camps was no indication of who would survive. What mattered was in each and every heart, mind, and soul. They were assuredly living in hell on earth, and each prisoner had to make the decision whether to keep walking or to sit down and surrender. In those conditions, even the guards had to make a decision to go on each day.

It works in our favor that the human spirit is resilient, and our instinct is to improve our lot, wherever we are. The best advice I have ever heard on this comes from Winston Churchill.

> *If you're going through hell, keep going.*

If you stop moving forward, you are unlikely to get out or to change your circumstances. It is hard to get somewhere better when you are not going anywhere at all.

Fortunately, you control how your situation manifests. Not necessarily the cold hard facts of your physical realities, but your ability to cope with and to do something to improve your outlook. You may not be able to change your circumstances immediately, but you can determine how you react to it. Choosing to view the world through rose-colored glasses is completely within your control and capacity. For starters, do not look back. You are not going that way. Your past shaped how and why you are exactly where you are today. It only dictates your tomorrow if you let it.

What thoughts occupy your head? How do you focus on your end goal? If you are clear on where you are going, you need to keep putting one foot in front of the other. Set and achieve small, achievable positive goals, and sooner or later you will make it through whatever hell you currently may find yourself in. It cannot last forever, and you **will** feel better. All things good or bad eventually must come to an end. So, if you are going through hell, make sure you are pointing in the right direction, and do not stop now.

A complementary tactic you can employ is the classic attitude of gratitude. When everything looks bleak, there is still room to find something to appreciate. On some days, it may be simply a kind word from a stranger or a hot cup of coffee. Notice something of beauty in your surroundings or the fresh innocence of new life. Try to notice and give thanks for at least three things each day. Mealtime is a convenient reminder time, whether you say a formal grace or just pause to whisper a thanks into the universe for something good in your life. When your day is particularly bad, seek even more to be grateful for. This practice will strengthen and give you fortitude to keep putting one foot in front of the other.

Sometimes nothing is wrong per se, but you are simply in a unique season of life. Personally, I struggle with all of the time and energy that my young family consumes, leaving me with little to spare for myself. I think through all the ways I may be able to free up and reprioritize some of my time. Where I can make small adjustments, I do. Regardless, I keep coming back to the fact that these early years are ephemeral. They will be gone forever before I know it. Sometimes I need to set aside my dreams of adventure for a few years later when hopefully they can join me. I saw my mom go through the same thought process in her mother's final months. Although Grama could not have joined Mom on her future

How to Get Out of Hell:

1. Face the reality of your current situation.
   Identify what is permanent and what is temporary.
   Fixate on where you can affect change.

2. Envision your happy place. What does "not hell,"
   or better yet, "nirvana" look and feel like?
   Do you need to do anything specific to get there,
   or just allow time to heal your wounds?

3. Craft a few small wins to start building momentum.
   Focus on getting through the next week, day, or hour.
   Commit to taking one baby step at a time.

4. Seek things to laugh about. Little joy moments
   surround you at all times when you stop to notice.
   Find something positive to be grateful for.

5. If you are facing the right direction, all you have to do
   is keep on walking. Do not give up!

Keep Moving Forward

adventures, Mom made similar tradeoffs. This is simply the season of life each of us is in at the moment. The benefit is worth the cost, being aligned with our bigger picture priorities.

Recognize what season of life you inhabit. Honor what you can and cannot do within the boundaries it imposes. Embrace the moment you are in, whether it be the craziness of infants, diapers, and sleepless nights or the final months of a loved one's own journey. Acknowledge that you will never get these moments back and make the most of them. Make your plans for other adventures when this season has passed, doing what you are able to do now to be ready when the time and season is right.

Hang in there and be persistent. Life is change and change is life. If you are going through tough times, remember that will change too. Nothing in life, except death and sometimes taxes, is permanent. Life is as ever-changing as a flowing river.

"The four words that can make a sad man happy, and a happy man sad?
'This too shall pass'"

~ Old Persian Adage

WHAT WOULD WATER DO?

Water offers us many lessons in perseverance. Have you ever studied moving water? Not just sat on the beach looking for dolphins, or cast a fishing line into a babbling brook, but deliberately watched moving water while it flowed down its path? For me, water is a teacher of persistence and tenacity.

The next time you watch water flowing in a stream, observe what it does when it encounters an obstacle like a log or a rock. The water always finds a way. It may go over, under, or around the obstacle. It may wear away the obstacle, or take it down the stream with it. Sometimes it circles and eddies behind the obstacle for a while before finding a way downstream. The water never stops or flows back upstream. It persists and finds the path of least resistance. Furthermore, water never takes any obstacle personally and wastes no energy brooding or planning revenge. Water never

over-complicates the situation, and it simply does what it must to keep moving forward along its journey.

Rocks are there for a reason. In the physical world, they live in the riverbed because that is what they do. In the proverbial world, rocks represent obstacles and trials. They challenge you to be more creative in your journey down the river. They serve to filter out those who are not strong enough to continue down their chosen path. Occasionally that is where the rocks live, and it has NOTHING to do with you. Most things in life simply are not about you. They really are not.

When you encounter rocks and other roadblocks on your journey down life's riverbed, how do you react? Do you spend all your time swirling in front of the rock, grumbling about how it is there deliberately standing in your way? Do you blame the rock for its mere existence? Do you put all your energy into trying to move the rock, or into trying to make the rock change into something else it is not? There are better ways.

Be like water. Look for the path of least resistance. It is the most natural thing on earth to do. Avoid leaping to the conclusion that the rock must be moved or changed. That may not be the best option; you may never succeed. Can you simply go around or over or under, and if not, why not?

Too many of us fear this most obvious of solutions because it seems like we are letting the rock "win." We jump to the assumption if the rock "wins" then we lose by default. Challenge yourself on this concept: Is the winning and losing all in your head? The rock could not care less. Most rocks in your life are not there to spite you. They are just there, and often are not even thinking about you. As Grama would say, "That's life!"

Ironically, the path of least resistance is not always easy. It does help you to proceed past the rocks you encounter along life's way, which is easier on the soul than getting stuck on a rock forever.

When I find myself getting wrapped around my own axle and losing sight of my own goals, I return to a simple thought.

> ***What would water do?***

It would be tenacious. It would keep moving forward. It would not take things personally. It would find a creative way. It would go with the flow, and it would never give up. When you are struggling with something, ask yourself first what you can learn from water.

Just as water follows the course set by its riverbed, it also changes the course of the river over time. Your environment changes you, while you change your environment. We are all connected to one another as human-to-human, but also human-to-environment. We are products of our environment and our environments are products of us.

Ensure you have proper perspective as you work through whatever your challenge is. Will the issue matter five hours from now? Five days? Five months? Five years? Invest yourself based on the full merit of the challenge. Remember that you are both powerful beyond your wildest comprehension and a mere speck in the universal scheme of things. Balancing the feeling of being all-powerful and infinitesimally small is a healthy tension.

As a recovering type A+ control freak, I have been trying to internalize water's simple lessons to go with the flow, while leaving what a beneficial impact behind. Some of us are born wanting to control every last detail to ensure perfect outcomes, while others have wiser ways to focus their lives. I was one of the former.

As I get older and wiser, I recognize that if I wish to keep my sanity and live a happier, lower stress life, I must choose my proverbial battles. I can go where I want. By allowing myself the grace to be less fixated on having to get there in one specific way, I find that easier happier paths present themselves. My way is not necessarily the only way or the best way.

I continually remind myself to focus on the big picture and to stress less over the minutia where it is unnecessary for me to do so. Fight the good fight, but do not be there when a fight is unnecessary. Deal with rocks as I encounter them, and move on. Rocks are not to be blamed for being where or what they are. Fair or unfair, they are just rocks.

If you are constantly fighting rocks, look for alternate paths that will allow you to get further down the stream without requiring you to take on that fight. Having said that, if your passion is in rock fighting, by all means, fight away! Please do not blame the rocks for being what (or who) they are.

Start with something small. For example, do you constantly struggle over who controls the television remote? Ask yourself if this fight means enough to upset your inner harmony. Regardless of what the fight entails, your primary question is: "What is it worth to me?"

Next, take it into your own hands to find the path of least resistance. Be careful not to fight solely because you can, and remember that it takes two to tango. The best way to end most struggles simply is to stop struggling. It is difficult to argue with someone who utters, "I agree with you."

Ultimately you will want to assess the two or three biggest things in your life that are interfering with you getting where you want to go. You then have two courses of action:

1 - Stop taking it personally.

2 - Do something about it.

Never wait for someone else to change the situation. If you want to start a new career as say, a life coach, but struggle to get your toe in the door, think through alternative paths. Look for meet-ups in your area that discuss becoming a professional coach.

Find someone who is already a coach and ask them to mentor you. If you do not have the right degree, consider applying for admission to a leadership coaching certification program, like the one Georgetown University offers. If you lack experience, offer free coaching sessions at a local community center. Seek out a coaching *community of practice* within your company or city. Your mission is to gain experience, while building references and clientele.

"I get those fleeting, beautiful moments of inner peace and stillness - and then the other 23 hours and 45 minutes of the day, I'm a human trying to make it through in this world."

~ Ellen DeGeneres, American Comedian

NOW SHHHHH...

How do we combat brain fog where we think in slow motion or scatterbrain where we think plenty fast enough, but cannot focus on any one thing for too long? How do we handle Great Aunt Mildred's voice telling us why and how everything we are thinking and doing is wrong? Part of the answer often lies in stillness and silence.

Call it prayer, meditation, silence, introspection, or stillness. Quieting one's mind seems like it should be such a simple task since we own our own minds, right? The difficulty is that our mind's eyes are naturally looking back at the past and forward to the future. With every thought we have, we look to the past to decide how to categorize it or to the future to decide where to go with it. Is this thing a friend or foe? Was it harmful historically, and will it hurt me later? Do I want to eat this food? Did I like it before, and will I enjoy it another time?

It is an automatic response to analyze what has already happened and project it forward. It is difficult to walk the infinitely thin line between past and future that constitutes the present. Fascinatingly, we physically live ONLY in the present making that thin line infinitely wide, but intellectually we seldom do.

The ultimate state of living in the present is being able to let go of the past which no longer exists and stave off of worrying about the future. If you find yourself dwelling on regrets, you are living in the past. If you are chronically anxious, you are living in the future. The present is where relaxation most commonly resides, whether it is because you love that which you are doing or because you are free from worry, anticipation, and dread.

Whereas the sympathetic nervous system automatically controls the fight or flight response when encountering a saber-toothed tiger, the parasympathetic nervous system returns the body to what should be its normal resting state after the tiger is fought off, killed, or escaped from. In today's crazy world of non-stop chaos and perceived crisis, it is difficult for many of us to take a step off the fast track to pause and breathe. Our sympathetic nervous system never quite shuts down. Our bodies are built to handle spikes of adrenaline and cortisol. They are not built for chronic overexposure. Modern life has become such a fast-paced, never-ending series of stressors that chronic elevated cortisol is believed to be one explanation for the increase in stress-related diseases over the past century. When these two hormonal responses never return to their proper resting levels, your body cannot help but get overwhelmed.

In his 1975 book, *The Relaxation Response*[13], Dr. Herbert Benson explored how just as you can trigger the Fight or Flight response, you can also trigger the reverse of it through meditation and living *even if briefly* in the present. He dubbed this The Relaxation Response. Common methodologies to get into a still, meditative state include focusing your mind onto an object, repeating a word or short phrase, or simply deepening your own breathing. While thoughts race through, you let them pass without reacting, telling them "not now, come back tomorrow," or watching them float off like fluffy clouds passing overhead on a blue sky day. As your breathing deepens, oxygen floods your system, your pulse slows, and your blood pressure starts to decrease gently. Often this is when thoughts can finally still for a few minutes - long enough to start listening to yourself without words. Some have said that in meditation and stillness is where man and God meet.

However you wish to think about it, being able to quiet your mind of all the incessant chatter will bring you the health benefits of relaxation, stabilized hormones, mental clarity, and focus. Give it a try for a few minutes a week, then a few minutes a day. Go longer if and when you are ready. For a few minutes, be still, be quiet, and be one with yourself. You are pretty awesome. Take a few breaths to yourself.

I clearly remember a Tuesday night yoga class from a decade ago. Upon settling ourselves in, our lovely instructor, Lorraine, encouraged each of us to set aside whatever was troubling us for the duration of the hour-long class. She assured the class that each of our troubles would be faithfully awaiting us after final relaxation concluded.

Earlier that evening, Husband (who at that time was not yet Husband) and I had been quarreling about "something of importance," though I have no idea anymore what caused the disagreement. Taking a deep breath, I took Lorraine's advice and allowed myself to let go of the irritation for sixty whole minutes.

The class both energized and relaxed me, and I felt the zen by the end. After the concluding Namaste, I had the idea that since I let go of the hurt for an hour, I could give it another hour of respite. One hour turned into two, then a day and a week. I never reclaimed that hurt. I hope he did not either because we never revisited the argument.

This lesson stuck with me and I share it with others when relevant. I know that a lot of my fretting and distress happens solely between my ears, and is neither real nor relevant. The more I can relive this exact moment, the more I can move through my day with inner peace. I choose what I will let upset my internal harmony and what I will let roll off my back.

Socrates: "What time is it?"
Dan: "Um, it's 2:35."
Socrates: "Wrong! The time always was, is, and always will be now!
Now is the time; the time is now."

~Way of the Peaceful Warrior[14], by Dan Millman

PART 2: ATTITUDE ACTION CHALLENGES

What's the Worst that Could Happen:

1. Identify a fear holding you back from something awesome.
2. Write down all your worst case scenarios.
3. Next to each, write down the impact of the worst case scenario. Will you die? Will you go to jail? Will you be publicly shamed? Will you break a nail?
4. Add a third column for how you could prevent your worst case scenario from happening or lessen its impact. If it happens anyway, how hard is it to recover?
5. Notice how many of your fears really are not that bad or even likely to happen in the first place.
6. Go start doing the awesome thing you were afraid of.

Surround Yourself with Winners:

1. Identify the five people you spend most of your time with.
2. How would you characterize them? Do they represent the YOU that you want to be?
3. What's missing that you might seek out? What's there that you might prefer to avoid?
4. Choose one attribute that you wish to reinforce (or reduce) within yourself, and identify one person who can help.
5. Schedule a meet-up with your potential new friend now.

Take Ownership:

1. Next time you find yourself in a situation that went wrong, observe your immediate reaction. Do you assign blame?
2. What could you have done to produce a different outcome?
3. If there is nothing, then let it go. If you could have acted differently, make the necessary apologies and restitutions, while making a vow to yourself to learn from your mistake.

Don't Believe Everything:

1. What have you been conditioned to accept as "that's just the way it is"? Is there a better, faster, cheaper, safer way?
2. What unspoken boundaries contain you? Start testing them. Is there something easy that might lead to a better outcome?
3. Check yourself on self-limiting beliefs. Identify at least three potential alternate resources to help reach your goals.
4. Go for those bananas - You just might get them!

A Time and A Season:

1. Recognize what season of life you are in.
2. Embrace the moment you are in, whether it be the craziness of diapers and sleepless nights, or the final months of a loved one's own journey. Acknowledge that you will never get these moments back and make the most of them.
3. Make your plans for other adventures when this season has passed, doing what you are able to do now to be ready when the time and season is right.

Let It Go:

1. Consider an interpersonal conflict bothering you right now.
   a. What if you chose to step away from the conflict?
   b. Is the only possible outcome one winner and one loser?
   c. If you cannot leave the concern unresolved forever, can you put it aside while you are not actively resolving it?
2. Try letting go of the hurt, frustration, or anger for an hour if you can. Try for ten minutes if an hour is too much to ask. Set a physical timer if you need to.
3. Observe whether or not you pick up the conflict again.

PART 3: (R) RESOURCES

Resource   noun re·source \ ˈrē-ˌsȯrs , -ˌzȯrs , ri-ˈsȯrs \ [15]

1a: a source of supply or support: an available means (e.g., your parents, trade partners)

1b: a natural source of revenue (e.g., oil well, dairy cows)

1c: a natural feature or phenomenon that enhances the quality of human life (e.g., a water source, rainforest)

1d: computable wealth (e.g., financial assets)

1e: a source of information or expertise (e.g., employees, mentors)

Word Origin: First known use circa 1611

CHAPTER 8: YOUR UNFAIR ADVANTAGES

Dear Brooke,

I finally know exactly what I want to do. While it's a relief on one hand, I'm no expert. I don't have the requisite knowledge... I'm smart and educated but ironically I'm the picture of incompetence. Why oh why didn't I pick a better major when I had the chance?! I need new education and training but the traditional route isn't practical for me right now. I have neither the time, the energy, nor the money to drop everything and go back to school. Where do I go from here?

GET SCHOOLED

I like to think about resources in the context of knowledge (or access to it), health, people, time, and money (or other valuable, tangible commodities). We first will explore continually increasing your knowledge. We will address health later because, like it or not, you are solely responsible for your body's welfare. Success is difficult to achieve when your body is unwell. Otherwise, to be successful you neither have to nor should do everything yourself. Knowing what you must build versus what you can buy is the lynchpin to deciding where to apply yourself best.

To succeed in this world, you have to be good at something, so please make it something you love and can profit from. This is Basic Marketability 101. Is your mad skill the ability to talk to and connect with people, e.g., can you sell ice to the Eskimos? Consider sales or public speaking. Do you love math and numbers? How can you convert that love into income? Are you a natural coach or teacher? Identify your target audience and subject matter that brings you the most joy and fulfillment, then find a way to begin on that path. Stop worrying about whether you are smart enough. Smart is nonlinear and skills can be learned.

What do you do if you are mediocre at whatever you love? Regardless of where you are in your skill set, you must continually invest in yourself - your skills, your experience, and your education. Adding credentials may benefit you too. Already a master? Keep growing; we can always improve our abilities to perform our skill or service of choice. Never tried it? Take the first step. Give it a try. Sign up for the class. Find a way to get hands-on experience. Nobody in this world is at the point in their expertise where they have nothing further to learn or innovate in their chosen field. This is both the curse and the joy of life. Someone else will always innovate a better way to do something, invent a new product, or fill an existing need in a newfangled way. How might you be that disruptor in your field of choice?

This presents bad news and good news. The bad news is you will never ever figure it all out by yourself living solely inside your own head. The good news is that over eight billion potential teachers, collaborators, customers, and critics are in this world today and available to help improve your craft. By reaching out beyond yourself to learn from and teach others, you will improve your personal impact.

Whatever you choose, commit to learn all you can to refine your delivery skills for peak performance. Experience and practice cannot be bought. You must lean in and invest your hours to become the best whatever-you-want-to-be you possibly can be. I anticipate your reaction. "I have a full life already, how could I find time to go back to school? Impossible!" Maybe it is time to redefine 'school.'

How excited we are to finally graduate!! Whether high school, college, grad school, or trade school, graduation for many signifies **"the end of learning."** It is a joyous day indeed! No more grades, lectures, homework, tests, or studying. The routines of the semester or quarter fall by the wayside. I remember being so done with school that I did not even attend my graduation ceremony for my master's degree. I could not get out of there fast enough.

The fallacy here is if we stop learning, we risk being no smarter at eighty than we were at eighteen or twenty-four. Life will test us, whether we prepare for it or not. Lectures are available everywhere when we pay attention. The answers seldom lie in the back of any textbook, and it behooves each of us to figure it out on our own without any published curriculum or set reading list. Where do we go from here if no established institution is telling us what to learn or how we will be graded? Watching new graduates join the workforce is fascinating. They experience culture shock as they realize you do not get grades every few months, and semesters never end. In the working world, there is no fresh start every few months. It is one never-ending course.

We sit squarely behind our own driver's wheel at this point. It is incumbent on us to decide which highway to take, which side roads to meander, or where to go off-roading. Some will crash and others will never take the proverbial car out of park. It is our choice and that can be scary. Continuous education is key.

Let your car become your Rolling University as Cindy does. Cindy is always on the road, traveling between home, clients, offices, CrossFit, etc. Most car sound systems have Bluetooth or USB ports to connect your phone, and they all have CD players or (I am dating myself here) cassette tape players. If yours does not, consider having one installed. Use your car time to learn something new. Find free and paid podcasts online for any interest under the sun, and check out audiobooks for free from your local public library, or using the Hoopla app. Cindy is always listening to something to expand her mind, give her new perspective, and challenge her own assumptions as she drives around Jackson, Mississippi.

To take your podcast learnings to the next level, share episodes you love with a friend. Discuss the topic. You do not require a formal study group setting to debate what you heard. You can chatter with others live or via text or any social media platform you enjoy. I found myself exploring anything from human longevity to space exploration and industrial agriculture in this fashion. The key benefit is that it makes me think deeper and differently, once I have others to bounce the ideas off of.

Reading and self-study offer other avenues to continue learning on a low budget. If you do not read habitually, or prefer only fiction, ease yourself into educational material slowly. If you commit to and read only ten pages of educational material each day, you will cover an average of ten to fifteen books each year. If you read that many books in your areas of interest for more than a year, you will be on your way to becoming an expert in your field of choice. This accelerates when you start to implement the different strategies and techniques the books introduce to your thinking. Slow and steady can win the race. Most people can read a page in less than two minutes. Invest twenty minutes a day to grow new bodies of knowledge in support of your future goals.

Lastly and most expensively, you can attend seminars and traditional classes in towns and cities of all sizes. Unless the Harvard or Stanford name on the diploma matters to you for what you are trying to achieve, choose any local university or community college. Dedicate the time and money to taking a class in your passion area. Want to learn to be a better photographer, artist, chef, welder, dancer, or acrobat? Take a class. Want to get a full degree and change your career? Put your all into the application process and enroll full-time.

Explore virtual courses and degrees if that is more your style. Online curricula abound, some of which grant credit toward degrees. In the past decade, traditional academia has disrupted itself with massive online open course (MOOC) offerings including edX, Coursera, and the Khan Academy which provide Harvard, Stanford, MIT, Berkeley, Yale, and other top-notch university instruction. Many classes require no tuition fees, though you must invest your time and attention.

Once you sign up for the class, do yourself a favor and put yourself into it with your whole heart, mind, and body. Were you the one who always sat at the back of the class snickering at the nerdy kid in the front row? Be that nerdy kid. She was onto something. Being in the front gives you the best view of the board or screen, allows you to hear and see the best, and cuts out the distraction of every other student in-between. You are investing your time and money into these classes. Why would you shortchange yourself with anything less?

Read the materials, do the assigned exercises, lean into the group discussions, and ask every question you can think of. You have paid for the professor's time. It is yours for the duration of the class. Use it and get your full investment's worth. Prepare for tests, but make sure you fully understand the subject matter. If you complete the class with an A+ but have not learned anything, the professor will not have cared that you wasted your own time and money.

The three primary learning styles are: visual, auditory, and kinesthetic. Identify how you learn best, and set yourself up for success.

Visual learners tend to learn by looking, seeing, viewing, and watching. They need to see an instructor's facial expressions and body language or active demonstrations to fully understand the content of a lesson. They tend to sit at the front of the classroom to avoid competing visual distractions. Often thinking in pictures, they learn best from visual displays. During a lecture or discussion, they tend to take detailed notes to absorb information.

Visuals thrive by watching live lectures, consuming DVDs or YouTube tutorials, reading books with diagrams, and white-boarding with their instructor or collaborator.

Auditory learners tend to learn by listening, hearing, and speaking. They absorb content best through lectures, discussions, and brainstorming. The underlying meaning of speech is interpreted by listening to tone, pitch, speed and other speech modulation. Silently reviewing written information does not help much, though reading it out loud does. Storytelling is a powerful learning tool for auditory learners.

Auditories also engage well with listening to live lectures, watching DVDs or YouTube tutorials, and white-boarding with their teacher. Podcasts are a powerful tool as are audiobooks, lectures on CD, and discussion or study groups.

Kinesthetic learners tend to learn by experiencing, moving, and doing in an active, hands-on fashion. They learn by exploring the physical world around them. They have difficulty sitting still for long periods and easily become distracted when trying to learn by simply watching and listening. Role playing and simulations are quite effective. They are best suited for on-the-job training, apprenticeships, and experimentation.

We retain approximately ten (10) percent of what we see, thirty (30) to forty (40) percent of what we see and hear, and ninety (90) percent of what we see, hear, and do. Every one of us is born a kinesthetic. The only way we learn is by doing. Adults have the acquired capability to learn via all three styles but are usually dominant in one.[16]

Children engage the most readily in kinesthetic learning with hard work and persistence. From learning to walk, talk, and ride a bike, they stay on the task at hand until they achieve their immediate goal. While all children naturally behave this way, my son exemplifies this trait. As a two-year-old, Little Man was obsessed with the alphabet. Every time we played outside, he pushed a piece of sidewalk chalk into my hand and insisted I write the full ABCs on the pavement. He traced each letter, and a week before his third birthday, I discovered him writing his name unassisted.

As a kindergartner, he decided to enter the school's talent show as its only hula-hoop artist. He practiced indoors and out with the intent of keeping that big ring spinning. When the night of the show arrived, I worried that my shy child might not emerge from backstage. To our delight, he took center stage proceeding to wow the entire audience with a stunning performance. As gasps and murmurs sounded around me, my face ached with the intensity of my grin. His tenacity and hard work paid off, with thunderous applause rewarding his efforts. More recently he sat down to learn how to tie his shoes. Nothing was interrupting his quest for a securely laced sneaker. After failed attempt after failed attempt, he started getting the hang of it. He persisted in his mission and completed twelve successful lacings before bed. Writing, hulaing, and shoe tying can be watched on video, lectured about, and demonstrated. With tasks of this nature, however, visceral learning only happens through doing. You cannot learn to play guitar solely by watching someone else do it.

Instruction is one way to learn, but according to the adult learning professionals, only 10-40% of our learning comes from actual classroom or lecture type settings. We need to bring out our inner kinesthetic and "get our hands dirty" by *doing* whatever it is we wish to be great at. We cannot excel at something without actively engaging in that activity. Malcolm Gladwell repeatedly cites the 10,000-hour rule in his book, *Outliers*[17]. Those who are top in their field put in the hours of practice, on top of getting lucky, being born under auspicious circumstances, and having the passion for whatever that field is. Avoiding hard work on the path is hard. You must put in the time to become - and stay - proficient at anything. This is mandatory both for perfecting old skills to stay at the top of your game and for learning new ones.

You can read all the books and watch all the demos you want, but until you actually sit your backside on a bike seat, you will never know how to ride a bike. For some activities, nothing beats actual practice. You must develop your own muscle memory, and no amount of money or wishful thinking can replace actually doing whatever it is you wish to become good at. You have to write your own lines of code. You have to practice your own French accent. You have to ride your own bike. There is no substitute for practice.

"We have to abandon the idea that schooling is something restricted to youth. How can it be, in a world where half the things a man knows at 20 are no longer true at 40 - and half the things he knows at 40 hadn't been discovered when he was 20?"

~Sir. Arthur C. Clarke, British writer, futurist, inventor, and television host

LEARN CHAMELEON SKILLS

The more you learn and experience, the more you know. The more you know, the more adaptable and well-rounded you become. The more adaptable you are, the readier you will be for the next adventure life throws your way. You become a chameleon.

Shel is one of the most amazing, adaptable, chameleons I know. She is an Audrey Hepburn model of open-mindedness, curiosity, compassion, acceptance, and exploration in how and where she lives her life and relates to others. Shel is the third in her family of eight children and was raised in an Iowa farming community. Her extended family includes several farmers, ranging from small organic operations to large agribusinesses. They grew up on a razor-thin budget with little material wealth, but boundless love and family bonds.

Shel knew as a child that her life would not be confined to her Midwest town. Once she was eligible, she joined the Marine Corps which presented her with the opportunity to see more of the world. From Iowa, she ended up in San Diego and became a California surfer girl Marine. From there, she enrolled in the prestigious Creighton University and pivoted her career to the private sector.

Later in the fledgling Internet days, Shel reinvented her professional self in the tech arena. She met a cool boy, and on an optimistic whim, packed all her belongings into her trusty old jeep and drove cross-country to settle in the Washington, DC suburbs with him. They married and set themselves up on a gorgeous country estate, while working in the Internet world, investing in real estate, art, and securities, and living a fine life together. They discovered and bought a breathtaking river-front cottage in coastal Virginia, where the only sounds you hear are wind, waves, the calling of the seabirds, and occasional jumping fish.

She earned her International Executive MBA at Georgetown University and found a challenging role in a prominent government agency. After several years, they decided to sell this estate, and now live the city life in a one bedroom apartment enjoying all the richness Manhattan offers with culture, food, art, and city living.

With every personal, professional, and geographical move I see Shel make, she leans into her new environment, making new friends at every turn. She is by no means naïve, but she seeks and finds the best in each person she meets. She looks for the good. She seeks to build a community around her, and she succeeds. Others cannot help but love her. She is kind, positive, interested, and interesting. An extensive reader, she remains in learning mode and is a willing participant in any discussion you choose to initiate.

Shel will go to the ends of the earth to help others, but she knows her worth and will not be taken advantage of. She has taken her lumps and bumps and she has learned from them while smiling and keeping a joyous sense of humor about her. With the wisdom of now five decades, she knows who she is. She lets the river of life take her down its course, while keeping her hand firmly on her rudder. She makes subtle improvements to the riverbed as she passes through it.

I admire Shel on many dimensions, and I will highlight two. First, she is status-blind, having lived both financially poor and rich lives. She passes no judgment on you for your net worth and is a charming combination of frugal in her expenditures and generous to all around her. She sees you for who you are as a person and judges you on for how you treat others.

Having lived rural, urban, and coastal lives, and having gained significant domestic and international travel experience, she is comfortable in any setting. Shel is married to a Vietnamese man, and she embraces his family's heritage as much as her own. She has friends of all races, religions, nationalities, politics, genders, and sexual orientations. She loves each person for him or herself and not their categorical stereotype. I asked her about this. She could not pinpoint where it originated. However, she said it was likely, "growing up in the Judeo-Christian tradition with beliefs that each creature was put on this earth for a unique reason."

Her natural approach to life inspires me to be a better person, to set aside my own judgments, and to try to find the good in all I meet. I am happier when I am near her, and I know others feel the same. No matter who you are, where you come from, or whatever baggage you own, you are part of her tribe.

The second reason I admire Shel is that she continually reinvents herself from a knowledge and skills aspect. She was in the United States Marines, earned her college degree later, then she was in the tech world. After returning to school for a business degree, she moved into the public sector. She is always reading and learning by way of books, conversations, and the media. She never stops growing or seeking to learn, to understand, and to expand her mind. She loves learning, conversation, and intellectual discourse. Shel thinks in terms of possibilities. She travels, and when she cannot, she reads and learns from those around her. She does not let fear keep her from learning and trying new endeavors. She cultivates a village around her and lets others in.

"We are all a sort of chameleons, that still take a tincture from things near us; nor is it to be wonder'd at in children, who better understand what they see than what they hear."

~ John Locke, English philosopher and physician

CHAPTER 9: DON'T GO IT ALONE

Dear Brooke,

I have learned a lot and picked up new skills, but now I'm battling the world with an army of one. I feel so alone. I'm not lonely - I have family and friends, but none of them is entrenched in this pursuit of mine. I'm admittedly torn between being a fiercely independent person by nature, while recognizing that I won't realize my full potential as a solo act. As a "raging introvert" I'm uncomfortable putting myself out there. How do I find my tribe while staying my own person and preserving my independence?

ON THE SHOULDERS OF GIANTS

In addition to formal teachers, also seek out informal ones. Mentors provide personal guidance and expertise from the vantage point of being someone who already achieved that which you strive to do. Mentors come in all shapes and flavors, and it is best to have many. Seek out role models who have skills and experiences that you desire for yourself and initiate the conversation to engage them in your journey.

At a previous company, I took a perceived risk. I reached out directly to Dave, one of my company's most senior executives to ask him if he would take me under his wing. I carefully selected someone I respect tremendously, for his intelligence and leadership, coupled with his energy, passion, and charisma. On top of that, he led the organization I hoped to join in a year or so. I had progressed quickly to the next stepping stone of my chosen career path. I believed he could help me grow and succeed in my current role, while also guiding me toward setting myself up for the next one. I took a chance, laid out all this in an email, inhaled deeply, and hit "send."

It took me a long time to write that email, not because I had any uncertainty regarding my request, but because I tried hard to articulate the win-win situation. I knew without a doubt what was in it for me, but how does one articulate to a senior leader what is in it for him to spend time mentoring someone several links down the food chain? On a grand scheme, all enlightened organizations expect their leaders at each level to grow and develop their junior staff. I felt awkward making the case that he should help me out because it was good for the company. He already knew that, and pragmatically, I did not report into his organization.

I felt self-conscious of what I wrote regarding why he might want to help me. No matter how many times I revised my message, it still sounded arrogant or pretentious. Mentoring others motivates me, but you cannot automatically assume it does that for everyone. Finally, in exchange for his mentoring, I simply offered my candor

on whatever topics he was interested in, commitment to work on developing that which we would discuss, and anything else I could do to be of assistance to him in the future. I hoped part of that would be in a future role working for him so I could kick some butt and be an asset to him and his team.

He wrote back less than an hour later, simply: "Love to! [His assistant] will set up!" I was OVERJOYED and had a smile on my face all weekend. We scheduled lunch for that next Monday, and I could hardly wait! It was worth taking the chance to ask. We continued meeting periodically for the next year until both he and I left the company for different opportunities. Mentors come and go as each season of our lives and careers evolve. While we have not worked together directly in over seven years, we occasionally keep in touch to this day. He writes an engaging blog *Dave-ologies*,[18] and I hear his voice in my mind as I read his words of wisdom. Mentoring comes in so many forms.

I repeated this approach at my current company, again with someone a few levels senior to me. His response was essentially identical, with the added twist of asking me for my feedback in return.

A few lessons emerge here, starting with the perceived risk of reaching out to others who may be further along in their careers. We are all real people, who more often than not welcome the opportunity to help others, and appreciate being sought out for our counsel. I know the higher I or anyone else succeeds in any organization, the less and less recognition comes freely. Knowing I have made a favorable impression on someone, regardless of position, boosts my ego. It feels good!

The question remains:

What was the underlying risk in asking for help?

The risk of someone not having time or interest in being a mentor? No big deal. They say no, refer me to someone else, and we both move on. Would I have been poorly thought of for seeking a mentor? Not at all. It is an established best practice.

A second lesson of course is the value of the network and the importance of building relationships. They will evolve over time, with some strengthening and others fading away. I cannot emphasize this point enough: You never know where a connection will lead in the future. We are inherently inter-reliant on one another. Life rewards those who give and receive help with an open heart.

Mentoring conversations can wander into deeply personal territory. From experience, the more open each party is willing to be, the richer the relationship becomes. By allowing vulnerability into the conversation, the further and deeper the conversation can go *on both sides*. By acknowledging that we do not know everything and that we can learn from others, or that certain experiences have profoundly affected our life view, the entire world of possibility unfolds.

One of the hallmarks of my style has been to want to show flawlessness to the world. I am deeply uncomfortable learning in front of others. I hate trying new talents on a public stage where my mistakes and failures can be exhibited. My happy path is figuring it out on my own behind the scenes so that I can be polished and confident when it is time for me to showcase my skills. This has at least three failure modes:

1. If I do not have others to help observe and point out my mistakes, I may be self-correcting in a suboptimal way. There may be superior ways to do things that I do not happen to stumble upon.

2. It may take longer to get to that place of perfection without feedback from others or others showing me how it is done.

3. It can be lonely. By trying to do everything on my own, I raise an interpersonal impediment when I create the perception of perfection. When others think I do everything flawlessly, they are less likely to be comfortable being

flawed in front of me. It creates a barrier between us, and decreases the likelihood of forming real relationships.

In any mentoring relationship, the more you can be real, the more you may get out of both sides of the relationship. At work, you do not want to present yourself as a hot mess. Keep it professional and focus on the areas you are seeking to develop while letting down your guard to get the most out of each interaction. I have been shocked at how positive my results have been. I suspect you will be pleasantly surprised as you engage deeper with others and realize the rewards.

In addition to opening yourself up for input, invest the energy in following through on suggestions provided by your mentor. This is easier said than done. I know I myself have not always been the model mentee. I have to give a shout out to Hari who has gone so far above and beyond my expectations as a mentee. He is my model for personal development.

Hari approached me at an office-sponsored happy hour. It was loud in the brewery where dozens of people were trying to be heard over the din of conversation and background music. Although we had worked together on a project a year earlier, he was nervous as he mustered up the courage to make his request. He shyly asked me to mentor him.

My first question of anyone who makes this request inevitably is, "What exactly are you seeking mentoring on?" In the corporate world, folks are often told to find a mentor, so they do, but with only vague ideas of why. The problem is that it wastes everyone's time if they do not know what they need. Unstructured conversations result and they are no better off than before we started.

Hari shared with me his initial thoughts, and we set up our first mentoring engagement. He arrived at the designated time with a written list of the areas he wanted to improve. We started at the top, and it took several sessions to work our way through it all, while new topics were added along the way.

What impresses me so deeply is how Hari takes action after every single meeting. Our sessions start with a debrief of what he tried from our last discussion, and how it worked out. We dive into psychology and how to influence any given situation. We replay the scenes, celebrate the wins, and talk through alternate courses of action when they did not go as hoped. Time and time again, Hari goes off to do the hard work of putting ideas into practice. He thinks about our discussions and evaluates his results. He makes mentorship a deliberate part of his success to an uncommon degree. Hari's success at work has improved. Interestingly, he reports that life is dramatically better at home too.

I am humbled that my words and stories are so impactful to him and that he has put so much trust into me. I feel this way about almost every person I mentor, formally or not. Perhaps I should not have been so nervous about asking those two executives to help me. It is possible that they also derive this same joy from being asked.

Surround yourself with people who have already achieved the types of things you want to do, then do it better. If they took twenty years to figure something out, springboard off the knowledge they share with you and accomplish it in two months. This is known as *standing on the shoulders of giants.* Remember to thank them for letting you stand on their shoulders, and above all pay it forward. Help others up onto your own shoulders. Being part of a network allows you to both give and receive freely and uplifting one another with your unique skills, knowledge, and offerings.

> *"No man is capable of self-improvement*
> *if he sees no other model but himself."*
>
> *~Conrado I. Generoso*

IT'S THE NETWORK, DUMMY!

If you know what your big dreams, goals, and passions are, ask yourself this question:

Who are the five people I need to ask for help unleashing this passion?

Your network produces a treasure trove of support. It is a mechanism for exchanging what you have, for what you need, to get what you want. Not only can others help with what is in their heads and hearts, but they also may be willing to share their own time and money with you for a mutually beneficial outcome. Beyond time and money, your network produces fresh ideas and sparks new thoughts to build upon old ones. It will give you new perspectives to find different ways to solve problems and get past roadblocks.

It is highly possible that you are unaware that someone else has already solved your problem. In the course of a lunchtime, friends who were venturing into a similar line of business solved two of Husband's stumbling blocks in Virginia simply by sharing what they were doing in Arizona. It cost them nothing, yet provided him extremely valuable solutions.

Your network gives moral support and reinforces your faith and resolve when the going gets tough. The more people you tell about your dreams and goals, the more they will hold you accountable to achieving them while helping you along the way.

The Association for Talent Development (ATD)[19] conducted a study on accountability and found the following:

Action

Probability of Success

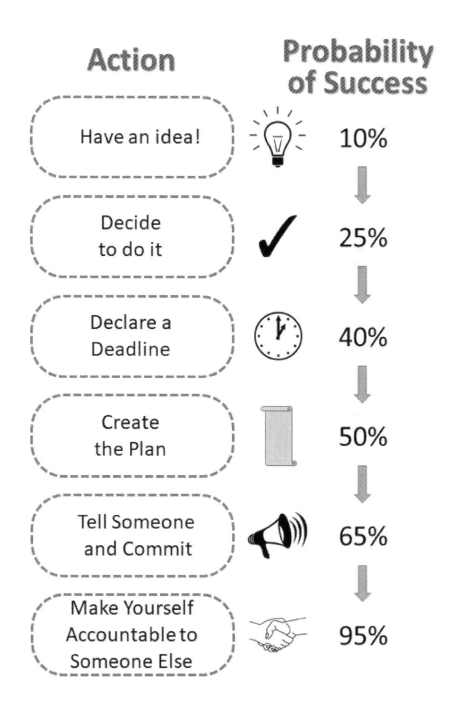

Action	Probability of Success
Have an idea!	10%
Decide to do it	25%
Declare a Deadline	40%
Create the Plan	50%
Tell Someone and Commit	65%
Make Yourself Accountable to Someone Else	95%

If you simply *have an idea* or goal, you are 10% likely to complete it. This rises to 25% if you consciously *decide* you are going to do it.

Once you decide *when* you will do it, your probability of success rises to 40%, increasing to 50% once you put a plan in place for *how* you are going to do it.

Telling someone you are going to do it and fully committing to it means you are 65% likely to achieve it.

The fascinating effect is if you *create accountability* with another person then the probability of achieving that goal is an impressive 95%!

Your network can help you psychologically achieve your goals while it helps you physically achieve them. As I embarked upon writing this book, Quincy also contemplated writing his. We challenged each other to publish by year end. Now each time we encounter one another, the inevitable question arises. "How is your book coming along?" It is a natural response to want to have progress to report back, and more work gets done as a result.

Whatever you are trying to achieve will only be done by working with others. The more you put yourself out there, the more you will get back. As an acute introvert, I know how difficult this can be at times. Regardless, you never know what you might learn from someone, what idea somebody else might spark in your mind, how you might touch another's life, or how it may all come back to you with future dividends in unexpected ways. Cultivate a human library. Instead of checking out a book, check out a person and hear their stories instead!

Who you know matters, but you do not need to be a schmoozer to succeed. For the first 38 years of my life, I mistakenly thought networking was about meeting with people and somehow pretending to be friends and all super-interested in them to frame a request. I misunderstood the point. I felt fake, phony, and awkward whenever I attempted what I thought networking was.

I had the good fortune to take a two-hour seminar that opened my eyes to the spirit and power of networking. Better yet, I learned how to give it a go. It is not about acting friendly in preparation to ask a favor at all, although both being friendly and asking for (and offering) favors are part of it. Networking is a deliberate activity. You and your new connection are cultivating a relationship with the hopes of helping one another out, directly or indirectly, immediately or in the future.

I cannot count how many friends' and colleagues' current jobs came not from applying cold to an online job posting but from a personal referral through their network. My own corporate opportunity came to me through mine. Alex, a friend and neighbor who used to work with me, proactively offered to pass on my resume to Raj, a classmate from his MBA program. I gratefully took Alex up on his offer and sent my latest version. Within a few hours I received a lengthy introductory email directly from Raj. We set up an interview, and I loved working on Raj's team for almost three years thereafter.

To staff up this same team, I pulled over two former associates who worked with me in another department. I built my new team using my own network. I found Patrick, a third team member, externally from a referral from a colleague who knew him through a friend of a friend. Patrick recalls having one conversation years ago with the first referrer that left enough of an impression to lead him to a new job at a new company eighteen months later. I constantly ask them to bring in their own friends whenever new openings become available because there is a fundamental underlying trust in the reference from people we know and respect.

On the entrepreneurial side, Husband's real estate adventure has exploded because of the networks he cultivated. He joined and ultimately became president of a local Real Estate Investor Networking Group (RING) in our town, and also became connected with a nationwide network of like-minded real estate entrepreneurs. They call themselves the Financial Friends Network, with the mission to help one another, as friends do, to grow each other's businesses. People openly share their business models, success stories, lessons learned, connections, processes, ideas, access to private funding, and most meaningfully, their friendships. The most common theme you hear when this group convenes is how the network changed their lives. As a tribe and an extended family, when one person succeeds, everyone else feels genuine happiness for them. The successful entrepreneur then turns it around, thanks the people who helped them succeed, and shares what and how they achieved so everyone else has the chance to replicate that successful strategy in their own market. The network convenes at any opportunity, ranging from holding mastermind events in Central America to celebrating a member's wedding in rural Kentucky.

Knowing now how to build your network, **use it**. Find out what others need. Share with them what you need. When you meet someone, ask them how you can help them achieve their goals. If they do not have an immediate answer, think through your contacts for someone who might be useful for them to meet.

If you are not comfortable asking your new contact if they can help with Problem X, practice asking them if they *know* and *would be willing to introduce you* to someone who can help with Problem X. Avoid pitching people on things. If you are looking for people to join you in an endeavor, share a recent success story and what you are looking to achieve. Ask if they know someone who would want to join in. They may be that someone, but if they are not, you avoid putting them in an uncomfortable situation.

*"Networking is all about connecting with people.
But then again, isn't that what life is about?"*

~ Jay Samit, American Businessman

ESSIE'S FULL CIRCLE NETWORKING WIN

My former teammate Peter asked if I would have a conversation with his wife. She sought a position within our company and wanted my counsel. It turns out that his wife is Essie, the lady who led the seminar on networking four years earlier. I gave them an hour of my time and counsel, requesting in exchange the presentation that she had given at the seminar. I would have given her my time and thoughts regardless for the sake of networking alone, but her materials just happened to be something I had been trying to track down for a while. I referenced her lecture from memory, but valued having her presentation to share more formally with others.

As we continued chatting, I learned that Peter and his wife had met Husband at a local RING event. That connection expanded into additional networking opportunities. They have seen their own real estate knowledge and endeavors grow, and to top it off, she landed the position that she interviewed for. Networking works, and Essie's act of giving the seminar on networking with no direct expectation of payback paid dividends for both of us four years later. Help may come from unexpected sources when you least expect it, especially when you are willing to take an interest and open yourself to others.

Networks take time and energy to nurture, but they can be manageable when you take a structured approach. I admire David for putting a system in place for nurturing his network. Once or twice a year he sends a personal email to me to say hi, give a quick update on his family and work, inquire a few specifics about mine (from prior correspondence), and reiterate his standing offer to be of service if there is anything he can do for me.

I always appreciate his notes and attempt to reply in a timely fashion albeit with mixed results on my part. He makes it a point to stay connected with the people he likes and respects, and I aspire to do more of that in my own network. Too often I find myself thinking of someone I care about, yet failing to actually put pen to paper, fingers to keyboard, or phone to ear to reach out. Although David celebrated his retirement this year, he is still reaching out to people that he wishes to remain in his circle.

The system recommended to me is to comb my list of contacts and identify 52 to 104 I deem particularly valuable. The measure of value may be different by each: some for knowledge, some for wisdom, some for their own network, some for sheer joy. By investing the time to write one or two personal emails per week, I can keep the relationship and the conversation alive with all 52 to 104 people. If you have something you'd like to share with many people (e.g., a brief update on your own life), it is ok to utilize copy/paste if that helps with your efficiency.

Not sure what to write? Provide a quick update on yourself, a few inquiries about your correspondent, and an article, link, or another resource that they would find valuable. The easiest gifts to give and receive are information, recommendations, and introductions. Provide your connection something of value in every interaction: a new idea or perspective, a recommendation, a referral, or an introduction. You aim to keep your old connections fresh and seek opportunities to create and nurture new ones. You will be amazed at what comes back in return. Karma is glorious in that way.

In 2017, I was invited to join an international conference on women in leadership. Networking was one of the subjects we explored heavily. It is a topic I am already familiar with, and although I know I can always do better, I thought I had it figured out. It was a wakeup call then when we took online self-assessments of our networks.

Our task was to identify twenty of our most impactful network members, then evaluate how they interplayed with one another. I was shocked to see that *by my own analysis* the bulk of my network was concentrated in the part of the company I had been with for only the prior thirty months. Despite having an incredible potential network, from two prestigious schools (one heavily international), and three Fortune 100 companies (one also heavily international), my network revolved around my current company and position. *What a wasted opportunity*, I chided myself.

I committed to renewing my efforts to re-engage with former friends and colleagues right away, starting with identifying with whom I most wanted to stay connected to. My criteria are simple: who do I like tremendously, who do I find particularly interesting for whatever reason, and who do I admire the heck out of. I could be more strategic around who might help my career, or be in a position of power, or whatever. For some people, these are crucial criteria. If you are building a business or building a movement, you need these power players in your network. You nurture your network in accordance with the goals you are pursuing.

For me, my personal goal is focused more on being surrounded physically and virtually by interesting people who possess diverse backgrounds and thought processes. In study after study, diversity of thought, background, and experience is shown to produce better results on endeavors in almost every dimension measured. It makes sense to apply it to our personal lives to ensure that we never get too stuck in our present way of thinking.

You can expand your network locally in many ways. Organizers extend public invitations to events daily on sites like Meetup, Facebook, Craigslist, and other online sites. Every community has opportunities to get involved, whether they are social, philanthropic, political, or entrepreneurial in nature. Your neighborhood, religious congregation, workplace, school, gym, library, and your local community center all offer great meeting spots. Several industries have professional societies, and entrepreneurs have various groups organized explicitly for building networks and creating commerce. Put yourself out there. Often all that is required to begin is simply showing up. You must be present to win.

Electronically, we have the social networks, with which most are familiar and I do not need to describe here. I will highlight

LinkedIn and Facebook as being two powerful choices for staying connected both professionally and socially. Every person will use these differently. I tend to connect with anyone on LinkedIn I know, whereas I try to limit my Facebook friends to family, friends, and neighbors with whom I have a more personal relationship. I know others use the two interchangeably and there is no right or wrong. The key here is to connect with people, go deeper than the highlight reel, then nurture the relationships on a periodic and ongoing basis.

If you are like me and the sizeable introvert population, networking sounds daunting and exhausting. It does not have to be! Networking is effective in one-on-one situations, and having tête-à-têtes may be more your style. Invite somebody to coffee or to take a walk, where it is simply the two of you. An adage about networking is "you should never eat alone." Something deep happens when people break bread together. It is the perfect opportunity to get a change of scenery from your workspace while forging or nurturing a connection.

Choose your tribe, engage with it, and nurture it with all your heart. Connections matter.

"The true value of networking doesn't come from how many people we can meet but rather how many people we can introduce to others."

~ Simon Sinek, British-American Author and Speaker

THIN THREADS OF CONNECTION

We are all connected in one way or another, and potential value can be found in every interaction. A frequent business traveler throughout my twenties, I burned the candle at both ends. When I flew, I always requested a window seat, preferably on the left side of the plane. Upon fastening my seatbelt, I promptly leaned against the wall and closed my eyes, desperately hoping for a cat nap or better.

Nothing annoyed me greater than having a Chatty Cathy seatmate attempting to strike up a conversation. One of my worst flights from an emotional point of view was when I was flying home on New Year's Eve to spend some time with my family. I had just returned to the country after working through Christmas day, which made me much sadder than I had anticipated it would. The relationship with my boyfriend was in serious trouble, and I needed time to regroup. I was exhausted. I was horrified when my seatmate pried into my business, grabbed my hand and started praying out loud for me. I contemplated jumping out the emergency exit.

As a full-blooded introvert, I was all about few, deep, long-term relationships, not three-hour flight friendships that would lead to nowhere and be a waste of my time. I genuinely felt and believed this. Mr. Dallas-Ft. Worth crossed over my line. My emotions were already raw and he just would not leave me be. It was AWFUL. I knew of many real-life examples of airplane meet-ups that led to more. One of my favorite roommates met her first husband on a plane. This was not for me. I simply was uninterested.

Scroll forward, and my perspective shifted. I cannot pinpoint why, but I did notice it along the way. I found myself in conversations with strangers in unlikely places, and I cannot to this day say why I engaged when I did. Somehow I started recognizing value in these exchanges. I still recall meeting Jill and Doug, two seventy-going-on-fifty-year-olds I met at the YMCA. I was being productive in a quiet little sitting area enjoying the free wifi. The next thing I knew, I was surrounded by a dozen senior citizens, socializing over coffee while I tapped away on my laptop. They completely ignored me, which suited me nicely while I attempted to get some work done.

As I wrapped up my to-dos for the day, I could not help but eavesdrop. I tried to keep a straight face while the ladies sitting across the table compared notes on the young men in their Speedos in the pool that morning. Apparently, the swimmers were quite pleasing to the eye. The old men egged the ladies on and I found it incredibly difficult to keep my expression neutral.

One lady bid her farewells to the other, leaving me with Jill sitting alone across from me. I half closed my laptop, remarking to her that I hope I am as awesome as they are when I am a little older. I do not remember the segue into the next part of the conversation, but we started talking about food, exercise, and general health. We ended up in an in-depth discussion about sugar, gluten, turmeric, and a host of food-related topics that happened to be top of mind for me at the time. Meanwhile, Jill's husband, Doug, sat down and joined the discussion.

Their uncanny resemblance to my grandparents (twenty years their senior) struck me, both physically and in the way they engaged a perfect stranger in conversation. When I mentioned an article I had read on sugar, in perfect harmony, they both declared "Poison!" in matching sing-songy voices. Yikes. Jill has fought weight and sugar since two gestational diabetes pregnancies fifty years ago. Doug cleaned up his own health when he retired in 2007. He decided he wanted to outlast his peers, which was incompatible with smoking several packs a day and hitting the bars every night. He just decided. Forty pounds lighter he looked and felt great. Jill declared she had boundless energy and felt like she could leap over this building. Wow. Although the YMCA is but a two-story building, I realized I did not feel that way. I wanted to learn more.

We connected on a few occasions, which included Jill gifting me books she no longer read and several article exchanges via email. She turned out to be a great resource on clean eating, a topic of emerging interest to me. I never anticipated this when she and her friends came into that sitting area. The only way I could have found out was by having a conversation and engaging with her and Doug. If you do not try, you will never know.

These sorts of interactions started happening a little more frequently in my life, which only could have manifested once I became open to receiving them. As they say, "When the student is ready, the teacher appears." I realized every interaction holds possibility. The person I engage may have a nugget with the power to change my life or perspective in ways large or small. Conversely, I may have something to offer to them that does the same. It does not have to be about a deep, lifelong relationship. Every conversation, every connection, every chance meeting may be that one flap of the butterfly's wing that starts a tsunami on the other side of the world.

Knowing where we are heading and where we want to go matters. Small influences along the way have the power to shift our direction by just one degree north or south. Using basic trigonometry, one degree of change makes the difference between landing in Amsterdam, Netherlands or Düsseldorf, Germany when you start in San Francisco and head east. Every degree matters. Engage with people, regardless of what you think you might get out of it. Remember that you may not be the intended recipient of the gift. Having said that, engage with people who are going places and doing things, not the ones who are standing still.

To be more of a go-getter, seek out other go-getters and engage like crazy. Seek like-minded and different-minded individuals. Test out your beliefs and theories on them. See what you can learn, and where you reinforce and revise your original hypotheses. Engage, connect, learn, and teach. It is part of the human experience.

When everyone is giving to us, it is mandatory in the grand karmic cycle of the universe that we give back, give forward, or both. Whether you feel compelled to do this out of the goodness of your heart, because you feel obligated, or because you simply believe that what comes around goes around, it is a healthy way to live. Many studies have shown that people who give, be it time, money, or advice, live longer, feel happier, enjoy lower blood pressure, and experience less depression than those who do not.

A study conducted at the University of California, Berkeley, studied people fifty-five and older who volunteered for two or more organizations. After normalizing for factors of age, exercise, general health and unhealthy habits like smoking, researchers found these active volunteers were forty-four percent less likely to die over a five-year period than non-volunteers. Similar results were found in a University of Michigan study of elderly people who actively gave help to others versus not.[20] Something happens biologically when we reach out and give of ourselves to others. Connections matter.

"Paradise has never been about places. It exists in moments. In connection. In flashes across time."

~Victoria Erickson, Author

PAYBACK TIME

> ### How can I ever pay you back for this?

Have you ever caught yourself telling someone you feel bad because you have received so much value from them, but you do not feel like you have given back enough in return? When were you on the receiving end of this comment?

The power of the sense of obligation is huge. Interestingly, we usually feel we need to give back MORE than we receive. Grocers who offer free product samples and real estate agents who provide cookies at open houses see the higher purchase rate of goods *and houses* consequently. Master marketers understand the power of reciprocation and obligation. Robert Cialdini wrote one of my favorite books, *Influence*[21], which explores this and five other key factors of persuasion. We inherently dislike the feeling of being indebted to others (human or entity), and we go out of our way to relieve ourselves of the perceived obligation. It matters not whether the concession was requested or the result of an unsolicited gift. The feeling of debt persists. To illustrate this, he highlights the Hare Krishnas who press flowers upon travelers in airports, refusing their return. The donations associated with flower giveaways far outweigh solicitations without them despite their trivial cost or whether they were wanted in the first place. Our wiring drives us to even out the score, and then some.

In April of 2008, I flew to Seattle to visit my mom's family. I had not been out to visit Grama and GrampO in a few years. The trip was long overdue. GrampO was turning eighty-six, and although he had suffered his initial stroke and was slowing down physically, the Alzheimer's disease that ultimately claimed him was not yet noticeable. GrampO was still mentally and emotionally present.

GrampO was one of THE most intellectual and accomplished individuals I have ever had the honor to know. An avid reader, thinker, and conversationalist, he led an extremely successful life between his family, friends, and professional accomplishments. As I hand washed the dishes one morning, GrampO lingered at the breakfast table as usual. He shared the thought that troubled him. While deeply thankful for all his life's successes, he struggled to know to whom to direct his gratitude. This bothered him tremendously.

I suggested he was doing well in the grand scheme of life since he had been meticulous at saying "thank you" along the way. More than that, he gave back significantly in return, from the graduate students he mentored at the University of Washington (UW) School of Dentistry to his patients in his private practice, to the study clubs he chaired and participated in, and to his family, friends, and the neighborhood where he lived for over fifty-five years. A UW alumni newsletter highlighted how one of his former students, Dr. James Oates, established a scholarship fund in GrampO's honor[22]. Dr. Oates thanked him for influencing his success, and by extension, helping those who will come after. GrampO paid it forward for most of his ninety-two years, as others he has helped do also to this day, several years after his death.

Life is tangled, and nobody is an island. Your successes in life so far are highly attributable to people who have helped you along your journey. From your parents who raised you and put you through college, or your closest friends who provided you counsel when you needed it most, or the manager at your first job who saw something special in you and took extra time to champion you. You did not get to where you are today alone. Be sure to make a difference for others too. Lighting another's candle doubles the brightness while in no way diminishing your own flame.

Mentoring is one of my favorite activities and a way I prefer to give back. At any given time, I actively mentor five people in addition to any direct reports I may have on my own team. We talk about anything under that sun important to them, and I try to share relevant ideas, advice, and lessons I have learned. Mentoring prompted me to initiate this book, after I observed two phenomena. First, I found myself telling the same stories repeatedly to different people, often regarding harnessing time and managing priorities. Secondly, as my children were subsequently born, I considered what I wanted them to learn. It was then that I realized personal and professional lessons often have interesting parallels. Be the shoulders others stand on.

Another favorite mentee is Sravanthi, who I met in the early 2000s. Over one memorable lunch, she walked me through a presentation she was particularly proud of creating. It was the final documentation for a specific type of assignment she had been anxious to do more of. This was her first major opportunity to fly solo while her manager was on vacation. She gave an excellent presentation and floated on cloud nine.

I felt deeply gratified by her success. While I carefully listened to her updates on the exciting things in her professional life, I observed her a little bit from afar. Her eyes sparkled, and her grin stretched from ear to ear. Despite Sravanthi being buried in work and the company navigating through choppy waters at the time, she shone from within. Seeing someone succeed, particularly when I had a teeny tiny part of it, is extremely fulfilling. Sravanthi and I connect periodically with healthy doses of feedback, encouragement, tough-love, honesty, and laughter. It is my way of paying others back, by paying it forward.

Not every kindness must entail a long-term relationship though, which brings to mind Jeff with the Yellow Shirt. GrampO was a huge road biker, and biking is a beloved pastime for me too. In the interest of getting in shape, I bought myself a new bicycle shortly after returning from my visit with him and Grama. It is a lovely road bike, and it must weigh less than twenty percent of the old bike I had been peddling since 1984.

I enjoy biking, and although Virginia is beastly hot in July, I decided to take one last ride before turning it in for its first proper tune-up. The tire pressure was low, and not having a good pump at home, I brought it to the bike shop for air. I told the helpful employee I would return my new bike before they closed at 8:00 PM so they could do the tune-up the next day. I also assured him I would purchase a pump when I picked up the bike so that he would not have to fill the tires for me anymore.

My plan was to pedal about six miles out, then turn back so I could make it to the shop before they closed. From where I departed, the six-mile mark was exactly on top of a bridge, with a lovely view of highway and trees everywhere. As I climbed the last gentle hill up to this bridge, I heard a pop and a hiss. I looked around for where someone was shooting leftover fireworks. As my bike started to ride funny, I realized I was that someone and the firework was my rear tire blowing out. Dagnabbit!! This was a new experience. I had never blown out a tire before, but of course not all new experiences are created equal. This one was not on my Bucket List.

I hopped off the bike and turned towards home. Six miles is only ten kilometers. I figured I could probably walk it (with my bike in tow) in about an hour and a half if I were brisk, hopefully making it back to the car before dark. UGH. This definitely was not in the plan, and now I was not going to reach the shop before closing time.

Enter Jeff with the Yellow Shirt. After I had walked half a mile back down the trail, Jeff with the Yellow Shirt slowed down and asked if I needed help repairing my tire. I accepted his offer immediately, thanking him profusely and silently giving thanks for friendly, helpful strangers. We pulled over to a little grassy area, and I told him I had a new inner tube, but no pump. I explained to him how it was a new bike, and sheepishly how I told the guy at the shop *literally an hour before* that I would purchase a pump tomorrow.

He chuckled as he showed me how to change the tire. I merely observed, but he talked me through each step so I could do it myself next time. When it came time to inflate it, he pulled out this slick

little CO_2 cartridge, explaining that it is quick, light, and portable, but also more expensive option than the normal pump. Voila! In no time, the tire was inflated and back on the bike. I carry some cash with me on my bike, and I asked if I could pay him to replace his CO_2 cartridge. He said, "Naah, just help someone else out in the future." My face must have brightened up as I told him I am a huge fan of paying it forward, and I certainly would do so. I thanked him again before we went our separate ways, never to meet again.

In this same vein, one of my current mentees pulled me aside recently to let me know she had taken a new role with a trendy tech company. Evelyn and I had been working through her career path options at her old company. Evelyn had been hitting roadblock after roadblock after roadblock with her boss and her desired career path. It was time for her to get a fresh start and pursue her dream of being a product manager.

In our farewell meeting, she reiterated how valuable she had found our time together. Furthermore, she was starting up a new volunteering assignment the following week as her way of paying forward my investment in her. She found the motivation to give to others from seeing the impact our interactions had on her own life and future. I could not have been happier for, or prouder of her.

When we connected a month later, she had new counsel to ask of me. We were keeping the relationship alive, transcending distance and company alignment. She went on to share that our relationship had been the best part of her time at her old company. I was humbled beyond belief and I reaffirmed my commitment to continuing my mentoring efforts. She went on to say that her current organization, wildly successful yet still immature as a young company, has almost nothing in terms of a structured mentoring program. She decided to be a part of creating one. Now she is active in *BuiltByGirls*[23], an initiative that matches young women and professionals for mentoring relationships. Mentoring and passing on the gift has become an important part of who she is.

None of us got to where we are today all by ourselves. We are all products of many other people's efforts. Payback those who have blessed you with their time and knowledge by helping others who need it. Consider paying it forward instead.

"You see, I do something real good for three people. And then when they ask how they can pay it back, I say they have to Pay It Forward. To three more people. Each. So nine people get helped. Then, those people have to do twenty-seven. Then it sort of spreads out, see, to eighty-one. Then two hundred forty-three... Then seven hundred twenty-nine... Then two thousand, one hundred eighty-seven. See how big it gets?"

- Trevor McKinney, Pay It Forward, 2000[24]

CHAPTER 10: TIME IS MONEY AND I HAVE NEITHER

Dear Brooke,

I have all these wonderful, grandiose plans, hopes and dreams for my life. They are truly amazing, but I'm stuck being unable to do anything about them. Between working full time, raising kids (oh my gosh, all of their ACTIVITIES!!), and keeping the household running, I can barely squeeze in a workout or relax in front of my favorite show. How on earth am I supposed to write my masterpiece, or get my advanced certification, or launch my side-business without being an absentee parent? I have neither time nor money, which seems to be a self-propagating issue...

BIG ROCK THINKING

First of all, recognize what season of life you are in. If you have young children, recognize that you are in a finite period of "long days, short years." These crazy, aggravating, magical, amazing years will fly by in the blink of an eye. Be present in these moments, and recognize that you will never get them back. Perhaps this is not the time to be launching new grandiose adventures, since truly you already are in the heart of one. This season will not last forever. I tell myself frequently that I can have anything and everything my heart desires. I just cannot have them all at the same time.

Having said that, I CAN make the most of the time I have in any season. "Adulting" is hard no matter what, and we often juggle more balls at any given time than most of us wish. We need to make sure we know which ones are rubber and will bounce back when dropped, and which are crystal and will shatter on impact. Guard the crystal balls with all your might, such as your children's youth or your own health. They represent some of your Biggest Rocks.

Proper prioritization coupled with keeping our WHYs front and center is the key to goal achievement. I love the story about the proverbial University Professor who conducted a famous demon-stration on priorities. This is our Big Rocks analogy.

The Professor set down a huge mason jar at the front of the lecture hall. Without a word, he filled the jar to its rim with Big Rocks. The professor then addressed the audience. He asked by a show of hands who was convinced from scientific observation that the jar was full.

When all hands went up, he dropped several smaller Pebbles into the jar, shaking the container until they settled into the gaps between the Big Rocks. For a second time, he asked his students if the jar was full. Most of the students raised their hands. The Professor smiled.

Without further ado, he pulled a bag of Sand from under the table and poured it into the jar, filling the space between the Big

Rocks and the Pebbles. When he asked again whether the jar was full, there was some doubt in the air... but still half of the hands went up.

Finally, The Professor took a growler of beer and poured it into the jar, over the Big Rocks, Pebbles, and Sand. The beer came to the top and for the fourth time, he asked his question. Having been tricked before several hands stayed down. The Professor raised an eyebrow. After confirming the jar indeed was full, he inquired of the point of the demonstration.

A student in the second row raised her hand. She declared with confidence,

> **If you try hard enough, you can always fit more in!**

Chuckling, he replied that while often true in student life, the point is to prioritize the biggest, most important items first, whether they be family, friends, health, career, etc. Had The Professor filled the jar in reverse order starting with the beer and ending with the rocks, he never could have managed to fit the Big Rocks into the jar. Furthermore, recognize that not everything can be a Big Rock, as the jar has a finite capacity. Know your priorities, align them to your WHYs, and slot them first in your life and schedule.

The direct analogy is to your life and interestingly, your calendar. The hours in your day are your jar's capacity. Although you can become more efficient at managing your time, you cannot create a twenty-fifth hour of the day. If you spend all your prime time (i.e., when you are most alert, creative, and available) responding to emails and washing the dishes, you will run out of time and energy in your day before you start on anything significant.

Conversely, when you block large segments of time on your calendar to drive forward on something exciting, you make sure it gets done up front. Magically, email still gets responded to. You indeed find time to chat with friends, eat a few times daily, visit the restroom, and run errands. You get much more efficient with the small stuff when you put the big stuff first. Interestingly, you may also realize that some small stuff does not need to get done at all. It simply falls by the wayside.

One student called out from the back, "Professor – what does the beer represent?"

The Professor smiled, replying, "No matter how full your life is, there is always time to have a beer with a good friend."

While we live too many states apart for in-person beers, I often call a dear college friend on the way home from work. My twenty-five-minute commute is an excellent time to stay connected. On one particular commute, she shared her usual set of woes, lamenting the difficulties of balancing life, work, family, health etc. Her particular concern was that anytime she focused on one area of life, things fell apart in the others. She was stuck in the snow - her wheels were spinning madly but she was going nowhere.

Her mother's advice was to lower her standards and shorten her to-do list. This counsel fell flat with Alicia, internalizing it as, "Do not be an achiever. Sit around and be lame." It certainly was not advice she was keen to take. My friend was receptive to alternative ideas, so I shared with her my model for prioritizing Big Rocks.

This particular conversation was on January 3 at the start of a fresh new year. We identified her most important categories in life:

- Raising her young daughters right
- Strengthening her relationship with their dad
- Getting grants funded in pursuit of tenure at the University
- Improving her overall health and well-being.

I encouraged Alicia to think about what two to four significant achievements throughout the year in each of these categories would satisfy her when she reached New Year's Eve. She should avoid overwhelming lists five miles long for each, identifying instead a critical few top priorities. These were her Boulders. Next, she was to identify what major milestones, achievements, activities or other wins would knock these Boulders out of the proverbial park. The key word here is **major** with an eye toward ruthless prioritization. These now were her Big Rocks for the year.

Once identified, she could start each day by choosing two or three daily actions to drive meaningful forward progress. She would commit to working on these Big Rock actions FIRST in her day. Email would be off, phones would be silenced and put away, and any other distractions would be minimized. If the action was in service to getting a grant application submitted, she would find a quiet place to concentrate undisturbed. If it was in alignment with deepening a family relationship, the TV may go off. If the activity was a family snuggle on the couch in front of a movie, phones would be tucked away to allow her to pay full attention to her family. Multitasking has been proven scientifically to be a farce,[25,26] and one's full attention is necessary to achieve anything great in life. This is not hard to do but it does require intentional action to commit. You can reduce distractions if you choose.

It starts with knowing what your Boulders and related Big Rocks are. Be sure you make people and connections part of your priorities. They help you achieve your goals in interesting ways, and friends bring joy and comfort. They trigger the release of oxytocin, one of our four happiness hormones.

It has taken me half a lifetime to pull myself out of my introverted shell, but I am finally recognizing the full value of human connection in the pursuit of joy and happiness. Whether it be lifelong friends or new acquaintances, the journey of life is better with travel companions. Set aside time for people, and when you are together - be present.

"For NASA, space is still a high priority."

- Dan Quayle, 44th Vice President of the United States

TAMING TIME: WHY TIME MATTERS

If you believe that time is not the most precious, most unique resource we have, ask the person whose time is coming to an end. No matter how wealthy, how smart, how powerful, or how persuasive they are, they cannot create more time. The twenty-four precious hours in every blessed day are ours to use or lose. Time also tends to be the number one reason others give me for why they cannot {fill in the blank}. It truly does not have to be.

Time is a resource and time is a dimension of measurement. As an operations analyst and efficiency expert, much of my corporate career has revolved around making processes better, cheaper, and faster: in two words, more efficient. I had a moment of crisis when I realized for activities we enjoy, the last thing on earth we want is efficiency. How would you react if your lovemaking was described as extremely efficient? You probably would not take it favorably. As I reflect on my career, it horrifies me to realize that I made a profession of speeding life up, as if the first one to cross the finish line is the winner. Indeed, unless there is an external constraint, we want awesome experiences to last as long as they can. We are in no rush.

So, why the industrial focus on efficiency everywhere? Clearly time is money. Less time means fewer people required. It means faster speed to market. It allows redirecting resources from slogging through yesterday's process to innovating the future. As humans, we want to reduce the duration of long, dull, or painful tasks so we may repurpose our time for activities that ignite our passions and create joy. Human history illustrates this. We continually innovate to accelerate tedious manual processes, freeing up time for leisure and creative pursuits.

While you can tap into *others'* time, two things to think about when managing *your* time are:

1. What are you going to devote your time to?
2. What are you NOT going to spend your time on?

How much does one hour a day add up to? You DVR *The Voice* so you can watch it in forty-five minutes instead of sixty. Congratulations on gaining twenty-five percent efficiency. What do the other forty-five minutes cost you though, and what is its return on investment? Forty-five minutes is a little over three percent of a day, or if you sleep six to eight hours each night, it is between four and five percent of your waking time. Watch this show or any other once a day, and it represents fifteen to eighteen days each year. What could you do to enrich your life and achieve your goals with an extra half month per year? Consider giving up one show per day for a month. Instead, dedicate that forty-five minutes each day to pressing forward on a favorite goal.

Connor built an entire business on creating virtual processes and compensating other people to do work he does not want to do for a reasonable fee. He profits from buying and selling properties he has never laid eyes on, in neighborhoods he has not yet visited, found by individuals with whom he has only virtually engaged, from and to people he has never met in person. The closing transaction is done virtually, using electronic documents and DocuSign. Connor does not accept payment by paper checks because he does not want to spend the time to go to the bank or do the mobile deposit from his home. Buyers wire funds directly to his accounts.

He has leveraged automation to add value to buyers and sellers, helping people sell and buy properties, making money without putting a dime of his own into any deal. It is an ultimate example of efficiency. He set a guiding principle around using routines, automation, and outsourcing to maximize his time by taking himself out of the process. It led him to a creative, brilliant, profitable business model. It allows him to invest his time in other ventures of his choosing. As I write this story, he is cruising to Jamaica while all this happens in his absence. He decided where he is not letting his time go, so he can as importantly decide where it will go. Perhaps it will go toward enjoying the next *The Voice* episode, though I highly doubt it.

What steals time from you? Do you let it go willingly, or is it silently slipping away? Identify what your time thieves are, and how you will reclaim some of that time to devote to your Big Rocks. Time is a nonrenewable resource. Use it or lose it.

"Fundamentally, the basis of all modern progress is the efficiency of labor."

~ Charles Schwab, American Businessman

WHAT ARE YOUR TIME THIEVES?

All the time, people bemoan, "I would love to do XYZ, but I just do not have the time." Last I checked, every one of us has access to the same daily twenty-four hours as Oprah, the President of the United States, and the teenager next door. How you choose to spend those hours matters. Assume we managed eight hours of good sleep every night (yeah, right, but work with me here!) and lived the standard corporate life. We would spend approximately ten hours commuting, working, and on lunch break during the workweek.

That leaves you sixty-two waking, rested, non-work hours to spend. Some of those hours will be spent bathing and eating. I do encourage both. You will probably need a few hours for obligations like paying bills and straightening up the house, though these can be automated and outsourced respectively if you choose to do so. After that, take a hard look at how you spend your time. Track the number of hours you spend in front of the TV, computer, or video games. Do you go to extremes to keep your house spotless or your yard HGTV-worthy? Do you pleasure-read or talk on the phone a lot? There is nothing wrong with any of these activities, as long as you are deliberate about prioritizing them against any other bigger life goals you might have. Remember that you have to fit your Big Rocks into your jar *before* the Pebbles, Sand, and beer, or the Big Rocks will never have the time and space to come to life.

If you choose to take the action challenge to record where your time goes, you may notice patterns on what steals your time away from you. Examine some usual suspects.

Willingness to Please and The Inability to Say No

Sometimes our time thieves are other people; specifically, those who are not in our Big Rock garden. Most of us want to say yes to others. We receive an invitation to have coffee and our automatic reaction is to try to arrange our schedule to accommodate it. Do we first ask ourselves if this is someone we WANT to share our time with? We are asked to volunteer by our school, church, or neighborhood and again we try as hard as we can not to say no. Friends call us, but then spend the time chattering about nonsense or complaining. It is natural to want to help, to appreciate being included, to live up to another's implied expectations and to avoid saying no at all costs. Unfortunately, sometimes the requester's top priority is not aligned with our own.

For many requests, we do not WANT to say no. Most of us want to spend time with friends and family or gift our time to worthy causes. These are wonderful uses of our time. The downfall is when we are asked, and frankly do not want to do these things, yet proceed to do them anyway. Maybe you bump into a casual acquaintance at the store. "Oh let's get together for lunch!" [Automatic response] "Sure, how about next Tuesday?!" immediately to be regretted. Another day the overbearing school volunteer coordinator "volunteers" you to bake twelve dozen cookies for the bake sale. You prefer to write a generous donation check and be done with it.

If you would cherish reconnecting with that acquaintance, or find joy in baking dozens of cookies then go for it. Enjoy every moment of it. When you are caught off guard and get backed into the instantly agreed-to and instantly regretted situations, it is better to have a plan. Practice not committing to invitations or requests at the first suggestion of people outside your priority zone. Craft a stock response about conferring with the calendar or your spouse, and see if the acquaintance ever follows up. It is possible that they are regretting the suggestion and subsequent commitment, too.

If volunteering is important to you but the request is un-appealing, frame up sincere responses around devoting your time to other causes, or come up with an alternate way to involve yourself. Consider different ways to support the current cause in a way more meaningful to you. For the chatterbox friend, practice steering the conversation toward deeper topics you mutually care about, or toward what is going well in her life and away from the negativity.

Ultimately, you must keep your eye on the prize. Is spending two hours with Annie Acquaintance a better or worse investment than spending it with other people in your priority zone? Would you rather bake cookies for three hours or put those same three hours into a cherished project? Time must be guarded more vigilantly than money because you can always find ways to earn more money. You can never earn more time, nor can you save or directly borrow it. Use your time wisely and learn to politely decline uninteresting requests that eat it away.

Digital Media and Screen Time

One of the most obvious time thieves nowadays includes digital media and/or screen time. Screens are particularly addictive because they are incredibly engrossing. Time evaporates without our notice while we are engaged. There often is not a clear end which by design keeps us under its spell: another link to click on, the next show queued up on the DVR, and the enticing "play again" button on the game.

Screens and digital gaming, in particular, stimulate the release of measurable amounts of dopamine. Several studies' findings on Internet addiction include reduced counts of dopamine receptors and transporters, stemming from chronic overstimulation of it. On the surface, releasing dopamine sounds like a positive thing. These activities are causing feelings of happiness and reward, but too much of a good thing is unhealthy. This dopamine release is stronger than that which can be triggered by human relationships, encouraging disconnection and isolation... and a craving for more digital interaction. The cycle perpetuates. You always need that next screen fix, and each fix needs to be a little bit stronger.

Multiple brain scan studies within the past decade have shown atrophy in gray matter areas of the brain (where "processing" occurs) in Internet/gaming addiction. Areas affected include the critical frontal lobe, which governs executive functions, like planning, prioritizing, organizing, and impulse control ("getting stuff done"). Volume loss was also seen in the striatum, involved in reward pathways and the suppression of socially unacceptable impulses. A finding of particular concern was damage to the insula, involved in our capacity to develop empathy and compassion for others, and our ability to integrate physical signals with emotion. Aside from the obvious link to violent behavior, these skills dictate the depth and quality of personal relationships. These are only a sampling of the impacts to the brain resulting from Internet addiction and related syndromes.[27]

The American Academy of Pediatrics (AAP) recommends no screen time for children under the age of two, and limiting it for preschoolers and school-age children, because "too much media use can mean that children do not have enough time during the day to play, study, talk, or sleep." according to Jenny Radesky, MD, FAAP.[28]

Among the AAP recommendations:

- For children younger than eighteen months, avoid use of screen media other than video-chatting.
- Parents of children eighteen to twenty-four months of age who want to introduce digital media should choose high-quality programming.
- For children ages two to five years, limit screen use to one hour per day of high-quality programs.
- For children ages six and older, place consistent limits on the time spent using media, and the types of media. Make sure that media does not take the place of adequate sleep, physical activity and other behaviors essential to health.
- Designate media-free times together (e.g., dinner or driving) and media-free locations at home (e.g., bedrooms).

While these recommendations were framed up for children, they apply to us "grown-ups" too. We need more time during the day to play, study, talk, and sleep, too. An Internet meme recently declared, "Cell phones bring you closer to the person far from you, but take you away from the ones sitting next to you." It resonated and I posted it on my social media account for a nice dose of irony. It is a fresh reminder to me to put the phone down and engage with the children in a live game of Rummikub, Memory Match, Chess, or Yahtzee.

I know for me, my time goes into overdrive while on my phone. Facebook, Slack, LinkedIn, and Pokemon-Go are the usual suspects. If you get me onto Pinterest, a magical time warp happens. The clock goes into hyper-speed, while I am looking at random DIY projects I know I will never attempt. Why do I go there in the first place? Hard to say. The answer probably depends on the time and day. After a friend shared how his teenage son and he had serious interpersonal conflict after the son's gaming abuse, I deleted my addictive Pokémon-Go and the non-educational games my kids had downloaded. They often grab for my phone and it is annoying on top of being unhealthy for them in the first place. I am fully aware that this youngest generation is growing up in a digital world, and they need to know how to use all the tools. I am determined that they also will know how to play and thrive in the real world.

I still chuckle at my friends Helen and Eric, who took their television into the shop to be repaired. They truly forgot about it. Last I checked, after four years neither had gone back to pick it up or replace it with a newer model. For me this is a little slice of nirvana. I would be perfectly happy not having a television in my house. I would get over missing the last season of Grey's Anatomy or Modern Family. This preference was vetoed by the rest of the household, so we strive to compromise on a reasonable amount of screen time.

Transportation and Waiting

How much time do you spend weekly going to or from somewhere, or waiting in a queue of some variety? How do you pass that time? To our earlier discussion, often the waiting time turns into screen time when *hopefully* not behind the wheel.

The most common of this potential lost time comes in the form of commutes - to and from work, shopping, sports practices, or mass transportation, waiting for planes, trains, and buses to get us to wherever we wish to go. Another big one for parents is the wait time during sports practices or kid birthday parties where our role is to stay out of the way. Waiting in lines is a third culprit - lines at the store, lines to get into a venue, hold times on the phone. These are prime multitasking windows of opportunity. Is your tendency toward killing the time, or putting it to great use?

The key question is how you can redirect some of this time toward achieving your dreams. Certainly, you will use some of this time simply to chill out and recharge after a long day. That is healthy and important. Sometimes we need to use the time to decompress with music, talk radio, entertaining podcasts, or simply silence. How can you leverage the rest of this dead time to start changing your life?

How you use the time will reflect your situation and surroundings. Are you alone where you can listen to a podcast for education or stress relief? Do you set your intentions for the day as you drive in the morning? If you are not driving, can you read educational materials or write to further your journey? Do you call someone you care about to catch up and deepen your relationship while you are sitting captive? If your spouse or children are in the car, do you use it for meaningful, connecting conversations, or are they all on their mobile devices while the radio blares?

It may sound strange, but I cherish my commute time because I consider it a rare slice of "me time" where I can use that time in various enjoyable ways. I have learned more from podcasts than I ever imagined possible. I have connected with old friends without interruption of children or my at-home to-do list. I have let my mind wander and stretch itself. I guard this time jealously, and I do what I can to preserve that oasis of mental time at every opportunity.

There is always some time lost simply in the act of commuting, however, that commute time can change our lives. The same will be true for waiting after being placed on hold or while sitting on the sidelines. Sometimes your job is to cheer wildly. Other times your kids probably want you to sit down, shut up, and let the coach do his or her job. Much of this manuscript has been written at swim lessons, basketball practice, and hip hop dance class. I enjoy watching my children learn their various activities and I keep half an eye on them. However, to be the best me I can be for them, there are more engaging times and places for me to give them my uninterrupted attention. Paying attention to their sports practices for me are negotiable. What is negotiable for you?

Procrastination

Sand and Pebbles are the favored tools of the *Procrastination Thief.* When I do not want to deal with the super big thing on the top of my list (looking notably like a Big Rock), I find a hundred lesser things to knock off that list. They look remarkably like email, housekeeping, closet reorganization, surfing the net, and a zillion other little pebbly tasks.

I will not argue that some of the Sand and Pebbles need to be done. Floors need to be cleaned, phones answered, emails responded to, airline tickets booked, shopping done. Relaxation is also a critical part of a healthy life, whether it entails playing games, watching a show, or reading a book. Where the difficulties arise is when these Pebbles crowd out the large time blocks necessary to dedicate to Big Rock progress. I have come home from work on many occasions where Husband has asked me, "How was your day?" and I have had to admit that it was extra mediocre. Barring the occasional day where I ran into a bad situation (mad boss, disgruntled customer, upset employee, etc.), those mediocre days tend to be associated with accomplishing relatively low importance activities. Simultaneously, the big-ticket items that by definition require time, energy, and mental investment to achieve never get advanced.

Large, meaningful activities can be daunting. They are scary, overwhelming, and often complex. Sometimes we do not know where to begin. They may not be as fun as the little things in the here and now, despite being extremely important to us in the grander scheme of things. If we wait until all the little tasks are complete, we will never start on the big ones. If we never start on the big items, we will never make progress on them. Our email boxes will be empty, our laundry and homes will be clean, our to-do lists will be checked off, but we will never tackle the amazingly big, scary, daunting, incredible goals we wholeheartedly want to achieve because we procrastinate our lives away. We live on "Someday Isle" and someday never comes.

Distraction

It is not uncommon to start your day with great intentions just to have one phone call, one email, or one person casually interrupt your day and throw everything off track. The crisis, problem, forgotten obligation, or tremendous opportunity was not on your short list of Big Rock efforts for the day. How do you handle this?

One proven method for preventing distractions is isolating yourself so that you are hidden from common disruptors for a fixed duration of time or productivity. Cynthia B. sets time-bound goals for herself to do extremely focused work, with a "carrot" to reward her concentration. For example, she may turn off all her distractors on her computer, and put her phone in silent mode and out of sight. She may book a conference room where she can close the door, or work in another building on campus where she will not be seen and interrupted. She cannot hide forever but she can protect blocks of time for herself, and block out the most common disruptors of her flow. After she has put in a solid hour, or completed specific tasks, then she rewards herself with a few minutes of talking on her phone, taking a walk around campus, or chatting with friends.

If you are working on something that has a different unit of measurement of productivity (e.g., pages of writing, number of items processed, quantity of products made, etc.), time itself may not be the best unit of measurement. When I am doing performance reviews for my team, for example, I work to cut out distractions for the full amount of time it takes to complete one review before taking a break. This type of incentive structure can help with both procrastination and distraction thieves.

Connor shared a ninja trick of his own. He sets his phone alarm to ring once each hour. When he hears the alert, he pauses to assess what he is doing real-time and checks himself on whether it is the most impactful thing he can be doing at that time. He course-corrects as needed and continues on with his day. This helps him concentrate on the priorities he set for himself and make the most of his time. Connor is hyper-focused on his time and efficiency, always seeking ways to shave minutes or seconds off work activities. This allows him to reclaim meaningful blocks of time to devote to the active life he loves: exercising, hunting, fishing, camping, and going to the lake with friends. These activities gratify him, whereas driving to the bank to deposit checks fails.

Perfectionism

A potentially more insidious time thief may be perfectionism. Besides being flat-out unattainable, perfection is not what it is cracked up to be. Recognizing how perfection hijacks your time is complicated. In your mind you perceive that you are merely doing the task at hand to the standard you have set for yourself. This is a tricky one because there are two valid and seemingly opposing schools of thought.

On one hand, if you always settle for good enough, you will never get to that elite echelon of AMAZING. No Olympic athlete ever settled for "good enough" because there is no such thing when it comes to being the top of your game in your given sport, profession, or passion. If you want to be the best, you have to invest tremendous amounts of time and energy while sacrificing many other things along the way. Libraries of literature exist on the ten-thousand-hour rule, as a minimum requirement to achieve mastery in your area of expertise. Gladwell explores and illustrates this nicely in *Outliers*, as have many others.

For two powerful lessons on time, consider Michael Phelps, the American twenty-three-time Olympic gold medal winner in swimming. In the Beijing Olympics of 2008, he won his seventh gold medal by one one-hundredth of a second. You cannot blink that fast. Arguably the gold and silver medalists were equally fast from a statistically significant point of view. By the rules of the race, Phelps won and now is on the Wheaties box. Almost nobody can tell you who won the silver or bronze medals (Milorad Cavic (SRB) and Andrew Lauterstein (AUS), respectively if you are curious).

In that game, time mattered, but it was not only the time on the official stopwatch. What got Phelps there? He started swimming at the age of seven, logging twenty-four years of pool time by the point of his fifth Olympic Games in Rio in 2016. At peak training times, he swims reportedly eighty kilometers per week, logging hours in the pool and the gym. If he averaged merely two hours per day for six days a week, that alone resulted in over 15,000 hours in the pool with an intense discipline and laser focus on becoming (and staying) the fastest swimmer in the world. Perfection mattered here to Phelps' Big Rock and would never be categorized as a time thief.

On the other hand, there is the warning to "not let great be the enemy of good," referring to how people will work on perfecting something with no end in sight. The book never gets published, the company's new flagship product never gets launched, the software never gets released. In search of perfection, it stays in prototype, revision mode, or draft. The moral of the story is to get your goal to good enough, by whatever the right standard for the situation, and move on to your next mission. Invest where it matters and beware of diminishing returns.

Ask yourself, are you striving for perfection in everything? Is your house immaculate? Is your closet ship-shape? If you start reading a book and decide you do not like it after thirty pages, do you feel obligated to finish it? Are you seeking perfection in every aspect of your appearance for the sake of what others may think?

There is a point where you can go too far when you obsess over perfection. My former group discussion leader, Millie Betts, once admonished us, "Perfectionism is the highest form of self-abuse." I have pondered this statement many times. I think what she means is it is unattainable and unable to provide a sense of accomplishment or satisfaction. You set yourself up for inevitable disappointment. To this end, the best we can do is decide when "good" is good enough for the Pebbles and the Sand. Free up the time, energy, and mindshare to dedicate a higher standard toward your Big Rocks.

My older daughter seems to already know this. She and I were making mini-pies in preparation for her seventh birthday party. I had never tried to make apple pies small enough to fit in muffin tins before. While the pie crust dough was behaving unusually well for us, it was not quite getting into the shapes and form we wanted.

I murmured that it was not going to be quite perfect, and in a bright and cheery voice, she reassured me, "Don't worry, Mommy. Just try your best!"

I was thrilled to hear such a healthy, wonderful attitude coming from sweet Baby Girl. We must be doing something right for her to think this way. Once again I am reminded of what each of us can learn from children.

Discriminating on perfection is complicated. There are deep psychological reasons that many of us (myself included) participate in the never-ending pursuit of perfection. It bears deep self-reflection to assess why each of us chases the unattainable. For me, in many ways, it stems from habits I was taught growing up.

It can be challenging to let go of the fundamental belief that perfection is always good and imperfection is always bad. When we apply it indiscriminately it can drive the best of us crazy. Now I that am a parent, I have been forced to accept the universal truth: one cannot have small children, an immaculate house, and one's sanity. I must choose two, and I have already committed to the children. I find it helpful to ask myself what is the worst that can happen if this or that is sub-perfect. It helps me prioritize. It also means my house is a bit of a mess.

Where is the balance? We have two different schools of thought, and in my experience we have room for both of these. It comes back to the concept of prioritization and goal setting. For your Big Rocks, go for the gold. Seek perfection and put the time into it. Invest the ten, twenty, or thirty thousand hours and see them come to life in ways you have never imagined. To find that time you will need to free it up elsewhere. The Pebbles and Sand are the best candidates for scaling back on delusions of perfection.

I was introduced to Agile at my former corporation, and it provides an intriguing, effective model here. The Agile concept in software development focuses short bursts of energy on creating and releasing a minimum viable product, later adding features, optimizing, and reworking it. Several industries are now using Agile, and there are even examples of families using Agile methodologies to improve their family dynamics. If you search YouTube you will get thousands of results.[29]

To provide a basic illustration of the philosophy, if we were designing a new car using Agile, we would first design and release the basic vehicle. Our Minimum Viable Product includes the Body, Chassis, Engine, Four Wheels, Steering, Transmission, Brakes. You get the picture. Once released into prototype, we then make it street worthy. Next, we may soup up the engine, adding more horsepower. Add power steering, maybe upgrade from manual to automatic transmission. Heated seats and steering wheel may or may not come next, then a moon roof and an upgraded paint job. At any time, you can choose to stop and live with what you have, or you can keep going. What comes next can be reprioritized at any point along the way. You start with good enough, then decide when to keep going, and when to stop.

Note that none of this is to endorse striving for mediocrity. That recommendation will never come from me. I advocate trying your best and continuous improvement, especially when it costs you nothing. Never be afraid to keep pushing yourself to go a little further, do a little better, try a little harder. In this way you continue growing with every opportunity provided that you do not do it at the cost of your Big Rocks.

Having looked at the various ways time slips away from each of us, how do we identify them? I put pen to paper to sketch out what my average ideal workday looks like. It includes:

- Getting enough sleep

- Waking early enough for morning routines (meditation, affirmations, exercise) and goal setting for the day

- Enjoying a non-chaotic, organic, whole foods breakfast with my family

- Taking the scenic route to work to listen to an interesting podcast or audiobook

- Having a hyper-focused and productive workday

- Leaving promptly to spend my return commute on the phone with a dear friend

- Eating dinner again with my family

- Shepherding the kids through a non-chaotic bedtime ritual

- Spending time catching up with Husband

- Being in bed at a reasonable hour, with time to read for twenty minutes while enjoying the scents from my essential oil diffuser.

The barrier between me and this ideal day is me and my ability to prioritize so that these things happen, without wasting time on Facebook, Pokémon-Go, Slack, Pinterest, Amazon, or the other millions of websites conspiring to take my focus away. I also need to ensure that I am striking the right balance between a tidy house and a cluttered disaster. My workday must stay on task, avoiding derailment from minor fire drills and hundreds of emails.

As you consider how much time perfection and continuous improvement are costing you, assess what returns you are generating. Where you find opportunities to reduce investments out of your Sand and Pebbles, you now have an opportunity to reinvest this time in the things that matter most to you. If you cannot let go of the concept of perfection, be kind to yourself and aspire toward perfect imperfection.

"On parenthood: Children + Clean House + Sanity ... Choose two."

~ Anonymous

OPM AND OPT

Success is not contingent on doing everything as a solo artist. More accurately, success is contingent on NOT trying to do everything alone. Taking it even farther, I would suggest that the more of the RIGHT people you include, the greater your success is likely to become. Resources surround us and each of us has access to our own unique combinations of them. I like to think of these as our unfair advantages, which we can and ought to use to our benefit. Other resources we will need to source from other people.

Resources are available to each of us in varying unique combinations of strengths and gaps. Success relies on managing your assets and rallying your resources toward the goals you have set for yourself. Note that some resources have to be balanced, because they can cannibalize one another. For example, the common trade-off between time and money. You spend all your time to make money (especially when young), then turn around and spend your money to reclaim time back in your life. Resourcefulness is simply the ability to meet and handle a situation given all the resources and unfair advantages you have available to you.

Sometimes you cannot do it all, no matter how hard you try. Part of the American persona is the Independent Individual who is self-sufficient and stands alone. While this sounds very noble, it also is a complete farce. We all need and lean upon one another day in and day out, like it or not. Other People's Time (OPT) and Other People's Money (OPM) are what make communities function, since we trade one or more of ours for someone else's every single day. It happens every time you step into a store. You do not have time (or possibly skills or the patience) to grow every food item you eat, and naturally, you trade your money for the farmer's or rancher's time. The farmers in turn likely do not have enough hours in their days to manage the entire farm, and they hire help to tend the fields, move the irrigation, or handle the harvest. The economic cycle goes on forever.

We each trade our time and money for OPT and OPM without thinking about it. I encourage you to do so more deliberately when it comes to creating your own success and achieving your dreams, fully knowing that this is where many of us become shy. The grocery store example is a pre-established system of trade. Initiating the discussion to set up the exchange of something of yours for something of theirs can be intimidating. With practice, it becomes comfortable and second nature. You have to ask for what you want from others, while being prepared to offer value in return. The key is making sure that what you are asking for is both within their power to give - and you have something to offer in exchange of approximately equally perceived value, now or in the future.

Consider what assets and unfair advantages you have at your disposal. Can you barter, sell, or otherwise monetize them? How might you trade what you have for what someone else has, be it time, money, or something more creative?

- Can you carpool with a neighbor to get to work or get your kids to events?

- Do you have a vacation home that you could swap with someone else for theirs? Could you swap your primary residence for a "free" vacation rental elsewhere?

- Do you have spare space that you are not using? Can you take in a roommate, rent it out short term (e.g., Airbnb), lease half of your garage to your neighbor with too many cars, or rent space in your side yard to someone who needs garden area?

- Do you bring your kids to the bus stop in the morning? Could you look after a few neighbor's kids and get them safely on the bus for parents who need just thirty minutes of coverage in the morning, in exchange for date night sitting another time?

- Do you need a business loan but cannot qualify with a bank for one reason or another? Does anyone in your network have private capital to provide at a compelling return rate, which you could secure in a manner to their satisfaction? Can you share the profits, where you do the work and they provide the financing?

- Can you rent out a boat or any other recreational vehicles short term, to help cover your own cost of owning, maintaining, and insuring it?

- If someone else wants to use your property for gardening or beekeeping, can you get paid in produce or honey? Can you get your property rezoned as agricultural and enjoy the lower tax rate?

There are countless ways to trade your time, money, and assets for others' in a mutually beneficial way. It requires a bit of creativity and the courage to approach them with a proposal, but lack of resources should never stop you from reaching your goals. Use your village to everyone's advantage, and be willing to give away value to create something of significance.

"Half of something is better than all of nothing."

~ Anonymous

CHAPTER 11: LET'S GET PHYSICAL

Dear Brooke,

I have grandiose plans for myself, but I'm tired all the time. I never seem to have much energy. How can I live the life I have in mind when I can't seem to get off the couch? I feel blah, stuck in this cycle of inertia. I'm exhausted, I have no will power against eating junk, and I know I should exercise… but I'm too tired. Does it even matter?

I'LL SLEEP WHEN I'M DEAD

Without good health, little else matters. You can be the richest, most famous, most loved or respected person on earth, but if you do not have your health, everything else becomes secondary. Once dead, you are simply history. You may leave a legacy behind, but you no longer have control or power over your future impact. It behooves us to mind our health, so we can enjoy every possible day with those we love, doing great things and making the world a better place while we are still here.

The theme throughout is that physical health cannot be outsourced. Only you can get the sleep you need. Only you can put the right food into your body or do those push-ups. You are the one living alone inside your head, despite all the other voices with which you share your headspace. It is your head, and you are your own bouncer for who gains admission. It is all you!

In addition to the ever-vital air and water, I consider three key dimensions of physical health, in order of how quickly their absence will kill me. Sleep comes first, with sleep deprivation being the second fastest killer after oxygen loss. Some brain cells start dying less than five minutes after their oxygen supply disappears. Working on the assumption we are not in an oxygen-deprived state, sleep deprivation therefore is the first macro factor that can kill us.

Setting aside the deadly impact of making mistakes behind the wheel or at work while chronically sleep deprived, we prevent our bodies and brains from conducting their necessary housekeeping while we snooze. It is killing us. Literally. In 2007 the International Agency for Research on Cancer (IARC) declared shift work (specifically swing and night shifts) a probable human carcinogen because of the effects of long-term sleep disruption.[30] This group 2A carcinogen classification resulted from the IARC's assessment that, "although the evidence for a carcinogenic effect in man is currently "limited," the evidence from animal experiments is already adequate."[31]

As we will not conduct to-the-death sleep studies on humans, we can look to rat studies to see the impacts of chronic sleep deprivation. A heavily cited study from 1995 concluded that "all rats subjected to unrelenting total sleep deprivation died, usually after 2-3 weeks. Rats subjected to selective sleep stage deprivation survived longer, but also died."[32] Perhaps it is not a coincidence that third shift is also called the "graveyard" shift.

Randy Gardner set the record in 1965 for the longest a person has ever voluntarily gone without sleep. At seventeen, he stayed awake for 264 hours (about eleven days) for a school science fair project. Other controlled experiments have seen people succeed for eight to ten days. I do not know how much rest Randy stored up before going into this experiment, whether forced wakefulness would have killed him on day twelve, or how long someone twice his age would have survived. It is an impressive feat given what we know can happen when the body is deprived of rest.

Culturally we wear how little sleep we survive on as a badge of honor, while it silently kills us. Social paradigms pass judgment on those who sleep more as lazy and idle. Ironically, the brain is extremely active during its sleep cycles. Many processes take place while we inhabit dreamland. These range from categorizing and storing new knowledge and memories to taking out the trash and clearing waste products from our brains. Human growth hormone is released, critical to both children and adults alike. Muscles repair themselves, cellular growth flourishes and blood pressure drops for the night. Sometimes we problem-solve while we snooze, evidenced by clearer thinking in the morning after a solid rest.

We know that sleep is important, yet so many of us are chronically sleep deprived. This has the same effect on the body as low blood alcohol content. Reaction times lengthen, judgment decreases, willpower crumbles, and our moods certainly are not Lil' Miss Sunshine. It is hard to live the life you want when all you crave is a nap.

I have found a sleep sherpa, in the form of health and nutrition expert, Shawn Stevenson.[33] He has a miraculous self-healing story of his own, after surviving a hip fracture at the ripe old age of fifteen. He had been a student athlete, competing heavily in track and field when his hip just broke. Ultimately he received the diagnosis of degenerative bone disease *and* degenerative disc disease at twenty. After several years of despair, poor nutrition, lethargy, and insufferable pain that prevented a solid night's sleep, Shawn took matters into his own hands. He started to claw his way back to health one habit at a time. Disregarding his many doctors' consensus that there would be no recovery, he dug deep and started experimenting on himself.

In addition to slowly creating new eating habits and reconnecting with his old companion "fitness" one painful step at a time, Shawn started paying close attention to what was happening inside of his body. He studied the endocrine system, looking at how hormones interact with one another. He also immersed himself in the world of micronutrients and the human gut bacteria biome. After nine months of intense focus on his health, scans showed that his herniated discs had almost totally repaired themselves and other discs were healthier. With that, Shawn shifted his university coursework to concentrate on health. Ultimately he opened a clinical practice to help others heal in the ways he proved possible. It was during his clinical years that he internalized how crucial the sleep component is in the healing processes.

I highly recommend checking out Shawn's book, *Sleep Smarter*,[34] which provides dozens of pragmatic tips to improve your sleep, written in a humorous and down to earth way. My key takeaway is that if we go back to how we slept in the pre-electricity days, our increased sleep quality will positively shock us. Picture your working day concluding when the sun goes down. Temperatures cool and dusk fades to black. The darkness suppresses cortisol and stimulates melatonin production. We crawl into bed shortly thereafter, cozied up next to a spouse or a sibling or two as children. A glowing red-orange fire is banked in the hearth, radiating residual warmth. The human touch stimulates oxytocin, magnified if extra cuddling is involved. Hours later, the rooster announces the dawn and we rise to a bright sun and vivid blue sky. Cortisol spikes naturally and melatonin production ceases. Caffeine is a relatively foreign concept and is completely unnecessary.

Today we stay up hours past sunset, squandering the four hours most likely to produce deep sleep. Part of this wakefulness derives from this morning's coffee. Did you know that caffeine has a half-life of almost six hours? Not only does it take roughly twenty-four hours to clear out of your system, but caffeine also stimulates the release of adrenaline and the fight or flight response.[35]

More likely than not, these late evening hours are spent cozied up with a screen of some kind. In doing so, we suppress the melatonin production and promote cortisol late in the day through electric lights and TV, smart phones, tablets, and computer blue screens. Whereas we can sleep contentedly with the red glow of lights, the blue lights scream "good morning!!" to us, triggering the wrong hormones. Once falling into bed, we invite all kinds of lights into our nighttime bedrooms and pile duvets upon comforters upon blankets, preventing a temperature drop from signaling bedtime. Alarms blare us awake, and we blearily reach for our coffee pots. The cycle continues.

I have invested a lot of energy in improving my sleep quality, and I am starting to experience positive effects. Without going into too much detail here, I strongly encourage you to focus on getting to bed earlier because every fifteen minutes counts. The few hours after sundown count the most for body restoration.

I have to keep reminding myself that before artificial light became widespread, human night owls did not exist. Mankind rose with the sun and set with the sun. Yes, we always had firelight (circa 125,000 BC[36]), candlelight (circa 3000 BC), and oil lamps (circa 4500 BC), but chronic "burning of the midnight oil" was unusual. While it pains me - a lifelong night owl - to go to bed "early", the reward the next day is notable. I am actively working on changing my sleep habits now, which will have the added benefit of helping me achieve my eating goals too, through improved hormonal balance of ghrelin (hunger) and leptin (satiety), better willpower, and fewer waking hours in the day to raid the pantry.

*"The cultural idea of sleeping when you're dead
will only accelerate the day that it becomes your reality."*

~ Shawn Stevenson, American Author

FOOD IS MEDICINE

Food is yummy. Food is fuel. Food is a joy. Food is easily imitated. Food is powerful.

I do not like food - I adore food. I love food. I dream of food. I love eating food, looking at food, making food, growing food, photographing food, and blogging about food. I have considered becoming an organic farmer, a caterer, a lunch lady, a food truck operator, and a food travel photographer. I have a personal unpublished cookbook containing over 250 of my favorite recipes, most of which I use repeatedly. I cook for others to show my love for them. Food and I have a deep, meaningful relationship that goes back for years. I have traveled the world and I eat almost every cuisine with joy and gusto. I have a stomach of steel, and little bothers me gastronomically.

My relationship with food took an unexpected twist when my youngest was not yet one. Her caregiver noticed she was getting red splotches around her mouth after Wee One ate, and she sent us pictures. We also noticed that her diaper was getting messier and messier, and we started wondering if the frequent vomit in her bed was tied to something she was eating. She was still nursing and my milk was benevolent, but sometimes after eating solid food or taking a supplemental bottle of formula, her little body went into distress. We consulted the best pediatric allergist in the area, and sure enough, she was allergic to cow milk, eggs, and soy. This was unexpected. We had never dealt with this before, and it drove us to start reading labels religiously.

Once in the practice of reading labels and looking for the known allergens, we also started questioning all the other additives and unknown words in the ingredients list. Never mind what we were avoiding feeding the baby. What were we feeding the entire family? I learned about all the various -ates, -ites, gums, lecithins, and carrageenan. Equally alarming were the sugars in all their forms and pseudonyms. At last count, sugar carries over sixty different names in the grocery store. By distinguishing sugar's forms, manufacturers can put more sugar in their products, while keeping "sugar" out of the top few ingredients, listing contents in order of quantity.

To be crystal clear, I love my sugar. Unfortunately, it is my worst addiction, complete with cravings, binges, and withdrawal hangover symptoms when I go cold turkey. Sugar's sweet siren song of temptation, reward, and consequence affects me on so many levels. Our ancient physiologies are wired to seek it out for survival. Although it is so abundantly available today, our bodies have not evolved in the last several thousand years to no longer pursue it. I see my older daughter also chasing this sweet monster, and it is a constant reminder that not only do I need to find a way to get past this addiction, but also I need to teach and model healthier eating for my progeny.

As I got deeper into learning about what is in our food, naturally and artificially, I discovered alarming lessons about what we are doing to our food supply. I discovered that not all eggs or potatoes are created equal. I learned, "it is an ear of sweet corn - I know exactly what is on the ingredient list - corn!" is not a reliable

assumption. Although I husked it, it does not mean that only corn is lurking within. It may have the pesticide and neurotoxin Roundup™ on the outside of it, and modified DNA within. The soil it grew in may be depleted of its nutrients. All the vitamins and minerals I expect to come along with the corn may not be there. Yes, it is an ear of sweet corn, but this ear of corn may have little resemblance to ears of sweet corn from my great-grandparents' days. The lineage of each piece of produce matters. This apple makes me healthier, while that one poisons me. What I feed my children matters and in turn, that which nourishes our food matters, be it plant or animal. We are all connected.

Interestingly, the connection expands beyond the molecular composition of the food we eat. I encourage you to look into local CSA (Community Supported Agriculture) and Farmers Market opportunities for sourcing your produce, meat, and eggs. By supporting local farmers, you are likely getting produce that has been grown locally, which supports the local economy. You avoid incurring the financial and environmental tolls of long distance transportation. You preserve the nutritional value of the produce which starts degrading from the moment it is harvested. It is picked riper, and gets to your plate faster without artificial chemical ripening. As a general rule, your food is raised sustainably and with fewer chemicals, which is good for you and for the planet. Lean toward organic and naturally raised to the extent that your finances permit. Google local farmers markets and CSAs to learn more about the options available to you - chances are they are closer and more accessible to you than you thought. Engage with the people growing your food, and learn about what is nourishing your body.

With careful label reading and food preparation, we were able to get Wee One past the worst of her food allergies. After three years of diligence, her skin tests came out clear, and we reintroduced the offending foods in limited ways. Soy is not a big part of our lives regardless, but when eating out we do not have to go to extremes to protect her from it. She loves cheese in many of its forms, and we allow her to enjoy it. While still cautious about eggs, we are relieved not to have to carry an EPIpen wherever we go.

This was a deep lesson on the power of food. Food can kill and food can heal. We are what we eat. Literally. If we do not put the foundational building blocks of our bone and cellular structure into our bodies, we are helpless to repair anything broken through normal wear and tear of the human body. Micronutrients matter, macronutrients matter, and all the additional chemical junk we put into ourselves matters. By eating a variety of nutritious foods, avoiding mystery additives, and listening to our bodies, we are giving our endocrine system what it needs to keep our hormones in balance. This provides our brains and bodies the nutrition they need to thrive, and gives ourselves the best chance to live a healthy, pain-free, disease-free existence.

Eat your vegetables. While your mama will be proud, do it not for her. Do it for you. You are solely responsible for what you choose to put in your mouth. While you can hire others to shop or cook for you, your mouth alone does the chewing and swallowing.

*"If you think the price of organic food is expensive,
have you priced cancer lately?"*

~Joel Salatin, American farmer, lecturer, and author

MOTION - USE IT OR LOSE IT

Although it has been said that abs begin in the kitchen and 80% of health is achieved through what we ingest, staying in motion is mandatory. The body was made to be active. Nowadays sitting is considered the new smoking for all its health detriments. Besides the recognized benefits of calorie burn, muscle tone, stamina, and hot bodies, motion is a required element to ensure our various bodily systems work as designed. Getting your heart rate up, breathing deeply, flushing out your systems with refreshing water, sweating out those vague toxins, and getting the blood flowing all helps keep you in proper working order.

I know my challenge is inertia. I have let myself get accustomed to being still, and I do not mean in the meditative, present way. My three children are always running a mile a minute, and I have to assume I also was that way once. Where did I lose it? I have no idea. I have never been particularly interested in playing sports, and my preferred exercise tends to be of an individual nature - walking, biking, swimming, yoga - except I never seem to make any of these a priority left to my own druthers.

Having said that, I recognize the importance of motion and try to work it into my day in small ways wherever I can. I love my wearable pedometer, and I am happy when I achieve my ten thousand steps for the day (roughly five miles of motion). I park on the opposite side of campus to force a few extra minutes of walking at both ends of the workday. I enjoy walking meetings with colleagues if the weather is neither too cold for comfort nor too hot to leave us sweaty and smelly for the rest of the day.

I have heard that we lose our fitness because we get older, but I believe we age more rapidly when we lose our fitness. There are countless examples of senior citizens who go from feeble to fit by starting slow and building up strength training over time. My favorite fitness role model is Ernestine Shepherd. At the age of 56, she and her sister, Velvet, started to work out together. After a disappointing shopping experience trying on swimsuits and laughing at one another, the two audaciously decided to become bodybuilders, despite being sedentary at the time. Although temporarily derailed when her sister died unexpectedly shortly thereafter, Ernestine pressed on to compete in her first bodybuilding competition at the age of 71. In Rome, Italy she was formally given the title of World's Oldest Performing Female Body Builder and secured a spot in the Guinness Book of World Records. Nine years later she still holds the title. Ernestine demonstrates that age is just a number. Through fitness and nutrition, she is in the best physical, mental, emotional, and spiritual shape of her life. For her, it all began with motion.

While not all of us are destined for or interested in becoming full-time gym rats, the lessons are clear when we watch what happens to those who stay active versus those who do not as they age. Certainly, unfortunate events happen, like my GrampO having a stroke after a lifetime of significant activity and fitness. It happens. We improve our odds, though, by moving our bodies regularly and deliberately.

I still recall posing a question about how much importance to place on our physical bodies since so much of what makes us unique seems to originate in our heads. I flat-out laugh at myself now, thinking back on that. The unbreakable connection between our gut, our immunity, and our psychology is gaining more and more supporting evidence every day. Our hormones move throughout our bodies, with brain affecting body and body affecting brain. The blood circulates without end, and what affects one body part may certainly spread to another.

As we are irreversibly connected to each other and the world around us, we are irrevocably connected to ourselves. So, take that walk, do some stretches, attempt a new sport, and play with your kids. You cannot outsource your push-ups. Only you can do them. *Future you* will appreciate it. *Current you* will notice that besides being in better physical shape, your stress level is more manageable and your mind is clearer. I certainly know that when I take care of myself, my brain fog dissipates. Not only can I think with clarity, but I am in a better state of mind. Everyone around me appreciates that. You too can increase your health and longevity simply by adding a little more motion to your day. Go take a walk, then come back here for your next action challenges.

"A body in motion stays in motion. A body at rest stays at rest."

~ Sir Isaac Newton's First Law of Physics, abbreviated

Also known as the "Senior Law" according to high school physics teacher Vince Mosconi

PART 3: RESOURCES ACTION CHALLENGES

Get Skooled for Free:

1. Learn how to use Podcasts. Choose a topic you love and listen to at least three while driving, commuting, or waiting.
2. Pick up an educational book of interest. Commit to reading at least ten pages every day.
3. Select a skill you wish to learn. Watch instructional how-tos on Youtube and practice the skill.

Networking:

1. Commit to meeting two new people and reconnecting with two existing people in your network monthly.
2. Practice asking indirectly for help, if direct is awkward.
3. Ask for introductions to others who may be of assistance.
4. Always find a way to offer value in return.

Mentoring 101:

1. Identify someone who is succeeding at your goal.
2. Ask if they are willing to take you on as a mentor.
3. Prepare an agenda for what you want from your mentor.
4. Bring scenarios you need help with working through.
5. Follow-through on at least some of their recommendations.
6. Pay it forward and mentor another. Ask in return only that they help someone else coming up the ladder after them.

Big Rocks:

1. Write your daily list of "To Do" items. Rank them by asking:
   a. What are my Big Rocks?
   b. What are my three key action items and deliverables for today to accomplish my daily/weekly/monthly goals?
   c. What do I/don't I want to invest my time in now?
2. After ranking, spend your time and effort on the top three items. Avoid distraction with Sand and Pebbles.
3. Reserve time to have a drink with someone special.

Track Your Time:

1. Track your activities with enough detail to get a sense for where your time goes.
2. Evaluate how you feel when you look at this.
   a. What surprises, disappoints, or delights you?
   b. Are you getting everything you want out of your day?
   c. Were you underestimating any time expenditures?
3. Identify where you have time hiding in plain sight (e.g., commuting, doing cardio, waiting in line).
   a. Find a podcast or audio book to learn something new.
   b. Nurture your network via phone or email outreach.
4. Identify where your presence is optional. If you must be only physically present can you:
   a. Bring a laptop, book, or podcast to use the time well?
   b. Squeeze in extra motion by walking or stretching?
5. Select one place you are willing to free up. Just say no.

Practice Saying No:

1. Assess the activities you get roped into. Is it too late to back out or renegotiate?
2. Craft a gentle refusal statement to use next time you get asked to do something you do not want to.
3. Practice saying it several times out loud until it flows easily off your tongue when you need to use it.

Digital Distractions:

1. Decide how much time you are willing to spend on media (TV, Internet, phone, podcasts, newspaper, radio). Are you willing to spend eight percent[1] of your waking life on it?
2. Measure how many times do you check social media.
3. Once you have set your limits, pay attention to what drives you there each time.
   a. Is it habitual and could you replace it with a healthy alternative?
   b. Is it triggered by something you need to be aware of?

Procrastination:

1. Declare one positive forward step you can take today to bring you closer to an important personal goal.
2. Do it FIRST before mundane chores or fun distractions.
3. Reward your own accomplishment with something fun.

Habits:

1. Identify at least one personal habit that irritates you.
2. Identify its associated trigger, behavior, and reward.
3. How might you avoid the initial trigger?
4. What is a more desirable behavior to react to that trigger?
5. What alternatives could replace the less healthy behavior to generate that same reward?
6. Give it a try.

---

[1] Assuming you sleep ~8 hours, eight percent of your waking day is 75 min. per day (doesn't seem like much), or one month a year (holy cow!).

Improve Your Sleep:

1. For one week, go to bed fifteen minutes earlier than usual.
2. For the week after that, turn in thirty minutes earlier. See how you feel.
3. Notice at what point you awaken naturally before the alarm ruins your morning.

In parallel, start making changes to your sleep environment.

1. Turn off or put away your screens an hour before bedtime.
2. Turn the thermostat down one, two, or five degrees.
3. Remove light sources that enter your bedroom, and replace green or blue clock displays with red ones.

Eat Cleaner Food:

1. Visit a Farmer's Market and engage with the sellers. Ask why the food they grow is superior to the grocery store.
2. Find out how they care for their plants and animals. Before purchasing a carton of eggs or cuts of meat, ask about the animals' welfare. Seek animals who were raised under the warm sun, in a pasture, without hormones.
3. Fill half to three quarters of your plate with produce before adding meats, starches, etc.

Move It:

1. Identify one small change you can make to reintroduce a little more motion into your life.
2. Commit to performing that motion daily for one month and observe how it makes you feel.
3. Do this regardless of whether you already have an active lifestyle, exercise regularly, or live on the couch.

PART 4: (E) EXECUTION

Execution noun ex·e·cu·tion \ ˌek-si-ˈkyü-shən \ [37]

The act of doing or performing something

Word Origin: First known use 14th Century

Chapter 12: Oh Yes You Can

Dear Brooke,

Being honest, I am excited but also terrified to death. I feel this is my time. I want to, but I just can't seem to move forward. There are so many obstacles blocking my way. I'm stuck in a proverbial traffic jam and I can't seem to make it to an exit to go a different route. I'm comfortable in my routines for now, so maybe I'll just stick with the path I'm on while I think about this for a while longer.

THE MAGIC OF "HOW CAN I ..."

When your Boulders seem out of your reach, one of the worst phrases you can utter is "I can't."

"I can't" shuts down the opportunity for possibilities and creative solutions. "I can't" closes the window for opportunity for ongoing conversation and exploration. "I can't" is a statement that even when it invites disagreement, puts everyone in the conversation in the mindset of negativity and finality. It is a synonym for NO without allowing the negotiation of possibility.

Instead, lead with "yes" despite not yet knowing how to make the yes happen. Replace "I can't" with "how can I?" and see what comes next. Ask yourself, "What must be true?"

To the example I offered in Part 1, if I want a new app of my own design, I have several options. I can give up on this dream - the least fulfilling option of all. I can hire someone to do it and find a way to solve the issue of intellectual property. I can give or sell my idea to someone else, to see the app made elsewhere. I can go to a class to learn how to program apps or teach myself online. Ten-year-olds are sitting in their bedrooms right now, working on equipment possibly older than they are, figuring it out. Surely with my age and experience in life, I have more resources available to me than a ten-year-old kid, right?

What that ten-year-old kid has that many of us have let go of is the will to make it happen, coupled with the willingness to learn, to try, and possibly to fail before succeeding. Furthermore, he or she is investing time into making this idea a reality. With the right attitude and the right investments of time, we too can be that app programming kid. It is all about creative problem solving.

For a different example, I have a friend who likes but does not love, her chosen profession. Although engaged, she is not married, and has no children, elderly parents, pets, or real estate. From my vantage point she is untethered. Her heart and dreams are elsewhere, specifically somewhere between working on a Tuscan organic olive farm and helping build new infrastructure in an African village. When I asked why she is here instead of in Tuscany, her eyes cast down, and she murmured she "just can't." I watched the light visibly fade from her countenance.

When pressed on it, she cited her fiancé. He feels obligated to stay near his parents who are starting to get up in years. He would be crushed if she were to go abroad, resigning her to a fate locked into Richmond, his family, and Corporate America.

I nudged her to think a little differently about it, in the vein of "how can I?" Could they go together now, before his parents needed them? Before they are married with children, which adds new considerations to any lifestyle overhaul plans? She started nodding and acknowledged he has been frustrated lately with work. He might actually consider it!

With a lightning-quick Google search, we found WWOOF[38] and several organic farms in Europe looking for unpaid interns in exchange for room, board, learning, and life experience. With new sparkle and hope in her eyes, she shot him a note with a few links letting him know she wanted to explore the idea that evening after work. Moments later he had already shut her down, stuck in his own "I can't" mindset, without talking it through or exploring the possibilities.

This time she was unwilling to give up quite yet. I asked her if she could go alone. She was not prepared to break his heart, and she felt that was not the right answer for her at the moment. We kept looking online for more information. Some farms require at least a six-month commitment, others much less. She has only three weeks of annual paid time off, but with her company, she can buy a fourth week with the next open enrollment opportunity in November. By timing it right, she could do eight weeks straight, four in December of one year, and four more the following January. Next stop: back to Google to find organic farming internships in Australia, South Africa, and South America where the growing season is in full swing that time of year. The hunt for a solution was on.

What else needed to be true? We brainstormed the questions she would want to answer. How much money could make this happen? How much time off from work could be arranged? Could she quit work altogether and generate passive income another way? How much knowledge or education is required? Are any frequent flier miles available? Was she willing to go alone, or would she need to recruit a friend to accompany her on the adventure? What new language skills should she develop before going? What knowledge would benefit her before embarking on this great adventure? Would small annual three to four week adventures scratch the itch, or does she need to completely overhaul her current lifestyle? What role does she need or want to invite her fiancé to play in this?

Instead of letting the conversation die with "I can't," she began asking herself "how can I..." The possibilities unfolded before her.

Several weeks later, I hosted a quarterly all-hands team meeting. We like to include a small personal development segment in the agenda to balance the day. Inspired by this conversation, I decided to try out this "I can't" exercise with the whole team. It was a little bit of a risk, and they could have reacted in a variety of ways. I was thrilled when everyone leaned into it. I invited everyone to think of a personal "I can't" and craft it into a "How can I." My objective was to help everyone think a little broader, with hopes of at least one or two people finding benefits personally or professionally.

A few things pleasantly surprised me, including one of my more analytical guys being stumped by the exercise. When I inquired what was going on in his head, he simply replied,

---

I just don't think in I can'ts!

I shot him a virtual high-five and encouraged him then to take one of his *"I cans"* and turn it into a "how can I go 10x bigger?" He started thinking about how he could one day own the Atlanta Braves.

Another surprise happened when I invited each person to share their thoughts with a partner if they were comfortable doing so. I was thrilled when they asked to share with the entire group instead. Openness and vulnerability presided, and we did exactly that on a voluntary basis. The lady who dreams of Tuscan olive farms shared her aspiration publicly. To her delight, another colleague spoke up. "Hey my grandmother has a friend who owns an olive farm. Would you like me to introduce you?" Her face exploded into smiles. "Oh yes, please!!!!" It reinforced the principle of putting yourself out there and asking the universe for the future you want. If you ask enough and put your own efforts behind it, at some point you will receive the aid necessary to get there.

You attract that which you think, talk, and obsess about the most. So without creeping anybody out, start obsessing.

"Impossible's not a fact, it's an opinion...
Things are impossible until somebody does it."

~ Tony Robbins, being interviewed by Joe Polish at the 2016 Genius
Network annual event

POSITIVE SELF-TALK

Now that you have started visualizing what you want and figuring out how it can be done, your next step is to remove any thoughts that are unsupportive to your goals. Whether cooking Beef Wellington or completing your first marathon, *you got this*! There are up to eight billion other people in the world who may jump at the chance to tear you down. Please do not pile on. Think kindly of yourself; speak kindly to yourself and about yourself. You are your own worst critic, but you do not need to be. You can love yourself and speak up on your own behalf while still owning your humility and not becoming or coming off as a pompous ass.

There is a generally accepted belief that our mind controls our body, whether it is the power of positive thinking, or the power of prayer, or the power of belief of all types. Henry Ford was spot on when he said, "Whether you think you can, or you think you can't, you're right." Our brains have the power to help us achieve the unachievable, and for this reason, positive optimistic attitudes are non-negotiable when it comes to success. Your brain believes the messages it hears the most often, regardless of truth, and impacts our body accordingly. The more positive, optimistic influences it receives, the more it will respond in kind.

Your own voice is the one you hear the most. Like it or not, it is your most influential voice in the world. Given this, should we not be telling ourselves the most loving, supportive things we can think of? I am not a trained psychologist, but I declare with confidence that the general trend in North America is to beat ourselves up. Perhaps it is to beat others to the punch, but regardless of reason, the more we tell ourselves *or others* how lame, weak, fat, stupid, lazy, boring, and otherwise mediocre we are, the more we believe it.

Fortunately, we have control over the most influential voice in our lives - our own. Our own voice, usually the inner silent one (though not always silent enough), is the one we hear the most words, thoughts, and ideas from on a daily, yearly, and lifelong

WHAT WOULD WATER DO?

basis. When we tell ourselves with enough conviction that we can achieve that goal, make that shot, nail that interview, or engage in that difficult conversation, our likelihood of success skyrockets. Conversely, when the inner dialog obsesses over how people do not like us, we are ugly, we are stupid, or we will fail at that thing we desire, the likelihood of these negative outcomes manifesting also skyrockets. We must be our own loudest and most persistent cheerleaders, visualizing our success, and talking ourselves into it with every waking moment.

We believe in ourselves so much that if we catch ourselves performing either above or below whatever we tell others our standard is, we quickly adjust to return right back to that threshold of expectation. You can observe this yourself in a wide range of situations. The golfer who performs three strokes below handicap in the front nine will miraculously go three strokes above in the back nine and come in right at handicap. The lottery winner who suddenly has a few million extra dollars will be economically right back where he was originally a few short years later. The B child who gets a few As at midterm gets Cs later on to end the semester once more with the B he or she expects. Conversely, the billionaire who goes bankrupt becomes a billionaire again a few years later. Our brain puts us right back where WE THINK we should be. Until we change our thinking, our results repeat.

Start by identifying the thinking patterns that are holding you away from your goals. Do you believe you can accomplish your dreams? What do you tell yourself about it? Do you tell yourself about all your limitations, or about how you are overcoming them? Do you start your sentences with "I want to {fill in the blank}, BUT {enter an excuse or self-limiting belief here}?" Do you focus on the possible, or on the roadblocks between here and the possible?

The more you practice telling yourself all the things you are accomplishing and working on accomplishing, the more your brain will get in line and help you get there. It is remarkably programmable to deliver exactly what you code into it. The secret is to code positive, can-do, exciting, supportive thoughts, and eliminate the contradictory instructions.

First, remove the negativity from your self-limiting, self-deprecating self-talk. For most of us, it is such a normal part of our internal chatter that we do not recognize it for what it is. Do you look in the proverbial mirror and see the best parts of yourself, or do you see the flaws? Do you see what it is, or what you want it to be? When you tell yourself "I wish … but …," your mind zeroes in on the *but* and believes that it is insurmountable. Start paying attention to this and identify what negative messages you tell yourself on a regular basis.

Next, replace the unsupportive thoughts with empowering ones. Did you catch yourself saying you are fat? Quickly counteract it with three or more positive actionable thoughts instead. I am working to be the healthiest me I can be. I am making great food choices. I am moving my body more today than yesterday. I love and accept me for who I am and what I am today. I am striving to learn, grow, and improve myself. I am beautiful.

I know self-doubt is real, and it is extremely powerful. Challenge yourself on all the things you worry about. So much of what you may be running from may reside solely in your own head. Now is a great time to rewrite your own stories. Start by asking yourself different questions. Instead of asking "who am I to …" flip it to "who am I not to …?" Instead of "why me?" flip it to "why not me?"

A year ago I started writing out morning affirmations to read silently, or more powerfully, aloud. They start with affirming how much I love mornings, while I retrain my night owl self to embrace the power of the dawn. They move on to compelling myself to exercise and find the beauty in a run, which historically has not been a favorite pastime. They wrap up by reinforcing to myself how deep and refreshing my sleep will be at the end of the day.

Recently, I recorded them in my own voice onto my music library. I listen to them in the car and during morning walks. I played some for Husband at risk of him laughing at me. He stayed quiet. Hearing your own voice repeatedly tell you how your life is going to be has the effect of making your subconscious believe it. This simple tool reinforces where you are going and how life is going to be. You are reprogramming your brain to get you back on your desired track should you deviate. Tell yourself repeatedly not only that you can do it, but also exactly how you are going to do it.

Nathaniel: "Sire, do you like yourself?"
Prince Edward: "What's not to like?"

~ Enchanted, 2007[39]

WHEN IS THE LAST TIME YOU DID SOMETHING FOR THE FIRST TIME?

I have struggled my whole life with wanting to learn in private. I dislike looking inept in public (imagine that) and prefer to learn whatever it is in private and then jump on stage with confidence. Success is a foregone conclusion. I wonder where I lost my children's ability to try something without worrying about looking like a fool. Kids always clamor, "Let me try it! I want to do it! My turn! Look at me!" When does this natural tendency fall by the wayside?

In our early years, we had new experiences all the time. From the first day of kindergarten and the first bike ride without training wheels to the first date, we were surrounded by firsts in our lives. Doing something new was pretty ordinary back then, and failure was always a possibility. It was the price we paid for knowledge, experimentation, and growth. All things considered, it was a pretty fair price.

Recognized by another name, we were surrounded by change. We kids held no fear of it. Furthermore, the adults around us seemed excited for us with each rite of passage, and we had no choice but to go along. New achievements produced cheers and applause, providing positive reinforcement for each subsequent milestone large and small.

Upon maturing, we settle into habits and routines. We tell ourselves we know our likes, and how we are going to live our lives. On one hand, great! It is wonderful discovering yourself and living the life that brings you fulfillment and joy. On the other hand, it is our nature to strive for a better life and improved circumstances. Change happens and helps us grow regardless of how uncomfortable the change is.

Once we stop growing, we start dying. We watch the world change around us, but we refuse to keep up. The world moves on without us. We need to recognize the stories we tell ourselves about growth and change and make sure they benefit our lives.

I am coming to the conclusion that there is something to be said about trying new experiences, and to heck with the *fear* of looking like a fool. This mental transition is far easier said than lived, but I am trying hard to shake off the discomfort. I was asked not too long ago to take on a new role at work. It is an area I am quite interested in, but not terribly skilled at yet. The team needs focus and leadership more than technical skills, which is good because I am much more adept at the former than the latter. Still, I need to learn how to speak intelligently in techie, and the best I can do is ask a thousand questions, and then a thousand more. It is an opportunity to practice vulnerability and openness, while trying to get past the uncomfortable feeling of not knowing what I am doing – while doing so on a public stage.

The bottom line is that I play the part of an extra in almost everyone else's movie. With that, I need to be much more concerned with what I think about myself than what everyone else thinks of me. Yes I need to be conscientious and add value to the team, but I cannot let fear stand in my way of learning something new and pivoting my career given that it is a move I chose to make.

Role models abound. I give mad props to Joyce, who at the age of sixty-five sold her flower shop and embarked upon a completely different venture herself. At the shop, she worked long hours seven days a week, and by all accounts lost her excitement for the retail business. Two years later, she bounces out of bed, excited for what new challenges, lessons, and triumphs the day will bring. While her friends are looking forward to slowing down and retirement, Joyce looks and acts twenty years younger. She is learning new skills, trying new activities, and rewiring her brain. Her best is yet to come.

Personally, I created a blog ten years ago, and eventually I finally began to rewrite those blog entries into this book. Sounds pretty safe, right? It took me over a year of thinking about each to get each of these efforts started and put the proverbial pen to paper. So far so good; nobody has laughed at me and why would they anyway? It certainly was less stressful than auditioning for The Apprentice TV program a while back – even without *The Donald* present. Maybe next year I will start my own company. It simply requires taking baby steps and trying something new.

How about you? Do you surround yourself with new experiences? Do you roll with the changes in your life, or do you fight to go back to more comfortable circumstances? How much do you allow yourself the opportunity to fail? What risk have you taken this week, and how far are you willing to follow it? How big of a risk does it pose anyway? I urge you to pick some crazy ideas and add them to your Bucket List, challenging yourself to actually do them.

There is never a perfect time for anything, which makes any time the potential perfect time. You can do it once you stop taking yourself so seriously. It starts with making a decision, and taking the first step. Give it a while then do it again. Wash, rinse, repeat. Take the second step, then the third. Success begets success, as you build momentum and start seeing progress.

"Just Do It."

~Nike Advertising Campaign, 1988

CHAPTER 13: THE HABIT OF WINNING

Dear Brooke,

I'm excited to get going, but anytime I start something new, inevitably I fall back into my old ways. I want to make exercise a habit, but after three intense weeks at the gym, I get derailed by a business trip or deadline. I get stuck back in my old patterns and never break through.

BRAIN HACKING

Hopefully, by now you have at least a general sense of your vision for your life, and your Big Rocks representing your top priorities. You believe in yourself and you are ready to make forward progress toward realizing your wildest dreams. You have assessed your day to know where your time is going, and what is stealing precious hours away from you. What is next?

The answer is unsexy, yet effective. It boils down to calendar management and having the fortitude to say no to your time thieves, then pivoting that time toward critical activities to achieving your dreams.

Easy-peasy right? We both know it is so much easier said than done. Knowledge is power, but knowledge alone fails to overcome the habits and routines we have hard-wired into our lives. Everybody knows overweight doctors and nurses who smoke. We know people in abusive situations who refuse to do what seems obvious to the rest of the world and get out of it. Everyone knows that losing weight entails more exercise and less food, yet we explore the topic over a pint of ice cream on the couch. What gives?

We need to examine our habits for the clues. Habits are a miraculous efficiency mechanism our bodies leverage to allow us to multitask without going into mental overload. If we had to think about every step our feet take, we would struggle to get anywhere. Which habits eat up your discretionary time? Where do you inadvertently choose to squander your time?

The goal here is to create this habit of winning, so each new adventure you choose to undertake is as successful as the first - if not more so. The brain is a wondrous thing; we are only starting to learn the extent of its capacity. In addition to using visualization and positive self-talk or affirmations to nudge it in the direction of our choice, we can harness its power of habit forming.

We can put our habit-forming brain to work for us, by carefully planting, nurturing, and cultivating the habits we desire. Habits in so many ways define who we are, whether we like the habits or not. Furthermore, they heavily influence who and what we will become. Habits drive us to perform healthy and unhealthy behaviors without having to think too hard about doing them. With enough repetition, these healthy, unhealthy, productive, unproductive, constructive, and destructive behaviors produce the outcomes of our lives. With enough healthy behaviors, our bodies and minds are likely to operate smoothly. Too many unproductive habits are likely to leave us unhappy and equally far away from living out our dreams next year as we were last year.

In *The Power of Habit*,[40] Charles Duhigg writes about the three parts of habit. First is the trigger, which is the thing or event that starts the habitual routine. Perhaps it is running into a person from your past, or smelling something reminiscent of your grandma's kitchen, or the daily 3:00 meeting at work.

Second is the behavior the trigger provokes. Does running into the person from your childhood make you fall back into childish behaviors? My college boyfriend called me out on this when he came to my home for Thanksgiving break. He observed that when my little sister and I were together, magically I was acting like a teenager again, quarreling with her over things that made no sense as a collegian. I was behaving in ways he had never witnessed back at school. His observation startled me.

Smells can be powerful - familiar smells from Grama's kitchen make you simultaneously relaxed and ravenously hungry. Without having started, the recurring 3:00 meeting puts you immediately on the defensive if the last months' worth of them have had reliably negative outcomes for you.

Finally, you get the reward. Our brains LOVE rewards! Quarreling with my sister was the old reward cycle for trying to best the other at whatever the situation was. The reward in Grama's house is comfort and a full belly with the serotonin blasts that come from each. The reward for going in on the defense to the 3:00 meeting is a less painful encounter than it otherwise would be.

The secret is to create habits that work FOR you and the goals you have in your life while overwriting those that work AGAINST you. They say there is no such thing as breaking a habit, but what can be done is overlaying newer, stronger habits. While there is debate, the rule of thumb is that it takes thirty to sixty days to firmly establish and entrench new habits. Over time, they only strengthen.

When you make a conscious choice to create the habit of winning, you reinforce the habit each time you deliberately make winning choices and winning actions. It gets easier with each subsequent, reinforcing choice you make to the point where making poor choices becomes uncomfortable because you are outside your carefully cultivated comfort zone of winning. Your brain tries to bump you back into the familiar patterns of winning. It is "just a habit" that you have formed.

Habits are by design mentally comfortable, including the bad, physically uncomfortable, or destructive ones. Everything we do is because we get a desired response in return. Action – Reaction. Ask yourself what you are getting out of your undesirable behaviors. It helps you identify the underlying psychology your rational self is competing with. Ask yourself, "what's it doing for me?"

Scientifically, habits are formed when you perform the same actions or behaviors repeatedly. With every instance, the brain lays down a micro-thin layer of myelin each time a specific neural path is followed. The more often you take the same path, the thicker and stronger the myelin pathway becomes. It is no different from how a cow path is formed in a field. With every cow that takes the trail, the more defined and easily followed the pathway becomes. Humans have been known to pave these pathways later because they're so well defined and packed down. Why not? The cows did half the work.

We can use this mechanism to our advantage by deliberately directing our "cows" (or actions in this case), down the trail (behavior) we wish to reinforce. Want to become an early riser? Force yourself to rise early until the habit you create makes it easy and unforced. Want to become a salsa dancer? Practice the same step combinations over and over again to create muscle memory. Want to improve your action orientation? Start with yes instead of no, then figure it out from there. Sometimes you will need to say no to competing priorities to make space for the bigger yes, but the big answer should always be yes. In short, you truly can fake it until you become it with enough deliberate practice and repetition.

Whatever it is will feel awkward and clunky at first. Learning to walk when you were one year old was awkward and clunky too. You persevered, practiced, and perfected it until you could walk without thinking. You created the myelin pathways and your body uses them automatically. Habits are one of our built in efficiencies so we can act without conscious thought. What other activities do you want to apply this magic myelin toward?

Just like water, your brain and body seek the path of least resistance. Sometimes you have to create that path. While it may be hard work up front, once created you will automatically seek and follow that path. That is what water does.

Cultivate your habits to help you use your time the way you want to - automatically. Remove the struggle and create the autopilot behaviors that help you keep your focus on your goals. It takes time and deliberate effort to form new habits, but with concerted attention and dedication, you can put your own brain's wiring mechanism to work for you. You will go with the flow, knowing the riverbed is pointed in the right direction.

"The chains of habit are too weak to be felt
until they are too strong to be broken."

~ Samuel Johnson, English Author

CHAPTER 14: MAKE YOUR PLAN; WORK YOUR PLAN

Dear Brooke,

I made my decision. I'm doing it. I'm climbing that mountain! But jeesh ... it's awfully tall. I'm awfully small. OK, starting to feel overwhelmed here. Maybe I'll just stay put. I know how to do that! Mountains are overrated ... and dangerous too. Yes, it's safer down here in the flatlands.

IDEAS ARE CHEAP

You know what you want to do and why. You have assessed and rallied your resources. You have everything in your head and maybe on paper. Why has nothing happened yet?

Sometimes all you really need is a good plan, broken into small enough pieces to make it easy to begin.

You now must take action. Ideas are easy, but worth diddly without execution to bring them to life. I use the Facebook lawsuit memorialized in the movie, *The Social Network*,[41] as a great proxy for idea valuation. The plaintiffs, Mark Zuckerberg's Harvard classmates Tyler and Cameron Winklevoss, claimed their idea spawned Facebook. After years of litigation and appeals, they were awarded sixty-five million dollars in cash and stock. This sounds incredible until you realize that at the time of the judgment, the value of the company was in the neighborhood of fifteen billion dollars. In the assessment of the court, the Winklevoss twins' idea was worth less than 0.5%. Zuckerberg's execution was worth over 99.5%.

So how does one "execute" anyway?

Once you know roughly what you want to do, it will stay a dream until you craft a plan and put that plan into action. If you are a natural project manager or agile scrum master, you can probably lean on your expertise. Identify what to do first, second, and third, then rally your resources against it. Start kicking butt and taking names. If you do not know what to do, ask others; watch, and emulate them. Corporate America offers some ideas.

In the corporate world, most organizations spend the first part of the year declaring and organizing around their imperatives, goals, objectives, key results, and a host of other concepts effectively centered around answering the question "how are we going to earn money this year while setting ourselves up to earn money for many years to come?"

Many will organize their efforts around the Balanced Scorecard concept, made famous in a book of the same name.[42] The notion is simple: you must adequately address your shareholders', customers', and employees' interests in order for your company to thrive in the long run. Ignore or underinvest in one or more of these dimensions, and you run a significant risk of the company falling into a crisis of revenues, talent, or valuation. In our personal lives, we also have distinct constituents (a.k.a. people who matter) and several dimensions to balance our resources across.

People who Matter

- Family
- Friends & Rivals
- Community
- Business Associates
- Mentors & Teachers
- Etc.

Dimensions of Investment

- Healthy relationships with other people
- A Healthy relationship with Myself
  - Body
  - Mind
  - Emotions
- My life's work and legacy
- My environment
- My finances
- Forces greater than myself

When everyone wants a piece of you, how do you prioritize? Taking the highest of high-level lessons from the Balanced Scorecard, the answer is that you must address all these dimensions and ensure that none is completely neglected. Oh boy.

Keeping it real, you cannot optimize on everything because there simply are not enough hours in the day. Optimize on one, maximize a few others, and ensure the remaining areas are good enough to keep you stable, balanced, and happy.

Force yourself to rank these dimensions if possible. Evaluate how you sorted your values in Chapter 2 (Staring into the Void). If too difficult, group them by the top two, the bottom two and the middle few, or something similar. You want to have a top, middle, and bottom group with no more than two or three occupying the top. The ones at the top will be your life's Boulders from which your Big Rocks emerge. You will invest the most of your energy into these, ensuring the others have at least enough attention to meet minimum requirements.

For me, my top three dimensions are my emotional (specifically my family), physical, and financial lives, each for different reasons. I am not going to claim that my actions are yet prioritized perfectly to optimize these, but here are the steps that I follow:

1. Define the goal for each.
2. Define the top level metric for knowing if I am winning.
3. Concentrate on the three most impactful things I can do to improve in each area.
4. Define how I know I am winning.

Here is an example for the physical health dimension.

I decided in 1998 that I wanted to "live a sparkly life" and I wanted my autobiography to be a romantic comedy adventure thriller. More recently, I decided that I want to live to see the entire twenty first century. For this to be possible, I have to be healthy by anybody's standard, and I have to do it for the rest of my life. Therefore, my top-level goal is to live past 128 years old with my full mental and physical capabilities intact. With today's advances in science, this actually may be selling myself short, but it is my starting target. I want to be that spry, endearingly crazy, little old lady who is a force to be reckoned with, whose kids, grandkids and great-grandkids have to keep up with.

What does this mean, though? We can start with beating the big killers, like cancer, heart disease, stroke, diabetes, Alzheimer's, and all the others of our current generations. Without going on too much of a tangent, there is a growing body of evidence that we are bringing all these ailments upon ourselves. While I am not taking on changing America's sedentary, Frankenfood, pharmaceutical culture here and now, I can take on changing that of my own and my family. I control what I put into my body through my own choices. I control how much I move my body. I control when I get into bed and mostly the things that interfere with deep sleep. There are half a dozen other meaningful areas of physical health, but these are the three I choose to work on first.

I have identified my top goal, a key metric (live past 128 years old with full capabilities) and the three areas I wish to focus on. My three areas now need measurements, and I can craft a first level goal set of objectives and key results for my physical dimension.

The three contributors are the most impactful things I can do today to drive toward my goal up top. These still are pretty daunting goals. We drill down to the next level, again focusing on the "top 3" in any given area. Take the example of sleep.

We could once again drill down to the next level of tactics, i.e., what are the three things I can do to "putz less" before bed, which requires examination of how my time disappears and then finding ways to reduce, optimize, etc. If these are the things standing between me and my goal of getting better, deeper sleep to enable me to live a better, longer, healthier, sparklier, life, then I need to craft my actions accordingly.

These all sound great, but may now be overwhelming. The next step is to identify which can be broken down further into micro-goals and tackled that way. Apply a little Project Management 101 and you are well on your way to achieving your wildest aspirations! What does Project Management mean? It means making sure you have the right vision, an appropriate action

Level 1

	Qualitative Objective	Quantitative Key Results
Goal	Live past 128 years old with full mental and physical capabilities	Age at death (128+) Mobile (no wheelchair) Legally competent
Contributors	Deep, Restful, Adequate Sleep	A weekly average of at least eight hours per day
	Put Healthful Fuel into my Body	Diet of Vegetable, Fruit, Nut, and free-range meats. Limit processed food or added sugars
	Movement Therapy (Exercise!)	A daily average of 10,000 steps or 20 minutes of deliberate motion

Level 2

	Qualitative	Quantitative
Contributor	Deep, Restful, Adequate Sleep	A weekly average of at least eight hours per day
Tactics	Turn off and put away screens in advance of getting ready for bed. Remove from the bedroom	Screens off by 9:15PM, stored elsewhere
	Physically get into bed earlier, curbing the putzing factor that eats up my evening	Be in bed by 9:45PM
	Turn lights off earlier	Lights out by 10PM

plan, the right resources, and the right prioritization in place to ensure that everything happens as desired.

As discussed in Part 3, everybody has some inherent unfair advantages of their own, and gaps they will need to fill externally.

Determining what resources you need, when you need them, how you will secure them, and then making it happen is at the core of setting yourself up for success. It starts with a plan and ends with execution. A plan that never gets acted upon is useless. Action without a clear vision or a plan may get you somewhere, but it may not be the destination you intended. Taking action is easier when you set micro-goals and start with baby steps.

"Have a bias toward action - let's see something happen now. You can break that big plan into small steps and take the first step right away."

~ Indira Gandhi, First Female Prime Minister of India

BABY STEPS AND NUDGES, BABY!

A micro-goal is a small accomplishment, achieved easily and painlessly. I employ them by simply looking at the daunting mountain ahead of me and identifying one to three tiny actions I can take today to make forward progress toward one of my Big Rock objectives. If I wanted to run a marathon but I am not a runner, these micro-goals may include buying quality running shoes and jogging to the end of my block and back. If too daunting, I could shoot for the end of my driveway. If I were already a runner, it might entail adding two extra minutes to my daily run, or a quarter or half mile. Micro-goals are about adding a little bit more to what you are already doing. They ultimately must align with your big picture.

The point of micro-goals is fourfold:

1. Make positive forward progress from wherever you are today.
2. Trigger a sense of accomplishment and pride. Enact the built-in motivator to set and accomplish more micro-goals tomorrow. This appeals to those of us who love to make lists and check off items.
3. Build momentum. Once you get started, your likelihood increases to do more than your original micro-goal required of you in the first place.
4. Introduce subtle changes that your brain and body will not immediately reject.

Think about it. If you are trying to get in shape, you might set the micro-goals to put on your exercise clothes, go outside, and walk five minutes. Once you are there, you are likely to do more than five minutes, but you have the built-in escape clause to stop after the first five minutes if you choose. If you are trying to write a book, you may set the micro-goals to sit down in front of your computer and write for five minutes. Chances are you will get into what you are doing and will put in twenty or thirty. If you need to get hundreds of weeds out of your garden, setting the micro-goal of pulling twenty a day will get it done. Why stop at twenty when you can do twenty-five? You are already in the zone with dirty hands. Give yourself a nudge.

There is a broader concept in neuroscience known as Nudge Theory[43], made popular in 2008 by University of Chicago's behavioral economist Richard Thaler and legal scholar Cass Sunstein. Thaler recognized that we do not always behave rationally. The general rule is that we will take the path of least resistance. In short, our inherent inertia occasionally can be used to our benefit, whether we want it to or not.

Thaler and Sunstein refer to influencing behavior without coercion as libertarian paternalism. Here an external party, like a government or company, tries to influence its targets to make good (in their assessment) choices, while recognizing that there is still full freedom of choice. Thaler and Sunstein ultimately defined:

> *A nudge, as we will use the term, is any aspect of the choice architecture that alters people's behavior in a predictable way without forbidding any options or significantly changing their economic incentives. To count as a mere nudge, the intervention must be easy and cheap to avoid. Nudges are not mandates. Putting fruit at eye level counts as a nudge. Banning junk food does not.*

The concept is that you can make small, unnoticeable changes that fly under your own radar yet drive outcomes that you want. People who eat on smaller dishes[44] or with pre-portioned snack packs[45] naturally end up consuming fewer calories without consciously choosing to do so.[46] Placing candy at grocery checkouts increases its sales, although living closer to the grocery store itself (vs. corner convenience stores) correlates nicely to healthier eating habits and consumption of more produce[47]. Part of it is sheer availability and ease of access. Marketers study behavioral psychology with a vengeance, and use it to drive their products to the front of your attention, or to nudge you to buy or spend a little more. You need to find your own nudges to counter any unwanted effects, since the draw to the path of least resistance is so strong.

Marketers are not the only ones applying nudges to the unsuspecting public. Thaler won the 2017 Nobel Prize for Economics, after his research in behavioral economics inspired the US Congress to overhaul the 401k Retirement Investment program. By making it an opt-out process vs. an opt-in process, participation in this company-sponsored savings program more than doubled. A 2015 Vanguard research paper suggested that this practice drove plan participation rates to more than 91% of workers from 42%.[48]

Amsterdam's Schiphol Airport was famous for painting house flies on their urinals. In providing a target, they saw an increase in accuracy of getting urine where it belongs and thus an improvement in the cleanliness of the men's restrooms. You can now purchase fly decals online for this specific purpose, if you wish to try this out at home. I am serious - check out urinalfly.com. Whether you prefer a housefly, a bullseye target, or rubber ducks for the kids, they have the urinal decal for you. It is social engineering at its finest - influencing people to do what you want, through slick design rather than lists of rules and mandates.

Sometimes the way you nudge someone forward is through one tiny step after another. Cynthia M. works with children with pediatric feeding disorders. Note that this is distinct from eating disorders, which stem from different origins. These children average two and a half years old, and for one reason or another struggled to learn how to eat solid food. For these children daily success entails getting them to try one bite of something new. The therapists do not go straight to cajoling the children to eat a grilled cheese sandwich. They start with one bite at a time, one food type at a time. Always start with the preferred and comfortable things. Make eating pleasurable, while nudging them to go a wee bit into the unknown. Make tiny changes within your comfort zone, and over time while your confidence builds, your comfort zone magically expands too. A child's beloved Pringle becomes a sour cream and onion Pringle. Once accepted into his repertoire, that sour cream and onion Pringle becomes a thin crispy piece of toast. After the crispy toast occupies the comfort zone, it may become buttered toast, then cheese toast and ultimately a grilled cheese sandwich.

This illustrates one example of how to continually nudge our comfort zones and achieve our goals with small baby steps, one day at a time. It also highlights yet another way we can learn from our children, whose daily growth outpaces our own exponentially. Life begins where your comfort zone ends. Be sure to scare yourself a little bit daily.

How do you eat an elephant? One bite at a time. Set the "just right challenge" for yourself – hard, but not *too hard*. Think about

what big dream you may have that seems so unattainable. Do you dream of wearing that little black dress in a size six, but you are currently sporting XXL sweats? Identify one small, manageable, measurable food or exercise goal you can accomplish today. Instead of getting lost in needing to lose twenty pounds, focus on losing one pound. Do that twenty times. Same outcome, but very different mental state.

Do you wish you had more friends in your life? Where might you go to get involved where other people you think you might like are hanging out? If they are at your church, how might you get involved to gain more exposure to them in a natural way? If they are all scrapbookers, how might you find an event online you could join? Frame up what you are looking for, and find out where others with these same interests hang out. Perhaps today's micro-goal is researching this from the comfort of your house. Tomorrow's micro-goal is signing up online. Want to learn a new language? Commit to practicing for five to ten minutes every day without fail. Surely you can find that small slice of time.

You have to put yourself out there in the universe, but you do not need to do everything all at once if it is simply overwhelming. Start small and let your own success beget success. Push your comfort zone bit by bit and you will be surprised with how much you accomplish. Start your own slippery slope to success. Once you get started and create momentum, you are predisposed through confirmation bias to keep on going. Nobody likes to admit when they are wrong, so they keep going down whatever path they have set out on. Use this psychological phenomenon to your advantage on your own psyche! Celebrate your wins along the way and have fun with it.

The first step is the hardest. Subsequent ones feel easier when you realize you not only can do it - but you already are doing it. Remember - if you never leave your comfort zone, you will end up exactly where you are today.

"The secret of getting ahead is getting started.
The secret of getting started is breaking your complex overwhelming tasks
into small manageable tasks, and starting on the first one."

~Mark Twain, American Author

MAKE A DECISION AND GO

At the end of the day, whatever "it" is, you indeed have to just do it. Stop talking about what you want to do and go do it. Stop thinking and preparing and talking about the things that will make you happy. Take that first step, then the second and third. Set three micro-goals that will take you toward one of your dreams and get started on them today. If the proverbial journey of a thousand miles starts with a single step, stop worrying about what shoes to wear on the journey. Go take that first step with your bare feet.

To achieve your goals, you must make the decision to do it. Several people asked me incredulously why I decided to start my first Whole30 dietary purge in the middle of the year-end holidays. There certainly are temptations galore, with the plethora of holiday parties, special elaborate dinners, and treats in the office. Husband and I were planning a cruise in mid-January at the time, certainly known for buffets and unending food and tasty beverages. His suggestion was to wait until we got past all this so I could enjoy myself and make the most of it all. A sage and sensible idea for sure.

If you are unfamiliar, the Whole30 essentially is extreme Paleo serving as a reset-diet. Many people have undiagnosed food sensitivities, and this protocol strips your eating down to vegetables, fruits, meats, nuts, and healthy oils. For thirty days, you eat no added sugars, chemicals, alcohol, grains, dairy, or legumes (including soy) - only whole foods in the compliant categories. The goal is to reset your brain, body, emotions, and hormones before you reintroduce these typical food offenders. You personally test how each affects your experience and decide whether you wish to keep them a part of your ongoing diet going forward.[49,50] It truly illustrates the notion of food as medicine, which we discussed earlier.

While it is challenging to adhere to such a restrictive plan, the side effects are amazing. Once you make it through the hangover and sugar withdrawal phases (which are REAL), your life measureably improves. My favorite Facebook post came from Stacey who wrote:

It is with a sad heart that I announce, after many years, Whole30 just isn't for me anymore. I've been experiencing terrible side effects, which include, but are not limited to:

- Bright skin
- Ability to focus more
- Great sleep
- Clothes fitting better
- Skyrocketing confidence

And to top it all off, I have to eat disgusting food, like this Seared Steak, Roasted Asparagus, Roasted Fries, and my Clarified Butter Robots [sic]. Who would choose to live like this?!??! Get out while you can.

Accompanied by a gorgeous photograph of her meal, it was one of the most heartily liked and commented non-viral post I had seen in a while.

The decision to start my own Whole30 the Sunday after Thanksgiving 2014 was the culmination of a few factors. First, I had been researching this stuff for about six months, so I had thought about before finalizing my decision. I thought I knew what I was getting into, more or less. Secondly, I had neglected to bring fun reading material with me to my relatives' house, so I had nothing of interest but my phone and *National Geographic* to read over the holiday weekend. This led me to embark on deep research (including the August 2013 *National Geographic* cover story on sugar) and planning. After psyching myself into it, I just decided to do it.

When someone *just decides* to do something, the likelihood of success improves. You cannot half decide or maybe decide. You must be all in. I decided to give it a go for one whole day, setting a timeline for myself. Up to this point, whenever I had tried to go a day without all the restricted foods, I had lost steam by mid-afternoon. I had not made the commitment to myself, so nothing changed. This time, I made my plan to eat cleanly for the day and I succeeded. Bolstered by success with this micro-goal, I decided to go for the full thirty days. I told my family about it, and asked them to hold me accountable. This time I succeeded not for a day, but for a month. It all started with making a decision.

The catalyst for making this wholehearted decision was waking up feeling stiff and achy after eating a large slice of cheesecake the night before. Whether the cheesecake was or was not the actual culprit is hard to know. What mattered is that I did not want to wait six to eight more weeks to start feeling better. That morning I decided and then I got started. It changed the course of my life in so many ways, on which I will elaborate in a future book.

I have a more recent story to share about Kelly. We worked together at my current company, and she became my closest friend there, going beyond being a chummy co-worker. I can be vulnerable with her without worrying about if she will think poorly of me or change how she considers me professionally. I admire Kelly for so many reasons. Her boundless energy and enthusiasm, her exuberant love of life, her professional perspective and success, and her overall coolness. She's thirty-something, living the Manhattan life with an abundance of friends and three pretty fabulous sisters. I cannot imagine what the holidays in her house must be like, with four Kellys playing off one another, laughing each other silly.

Kelly has had a stellar career, working her way steadily up the corporate ladder through a combination of being smart and innovative, working hard, and cultivating an attitude that propels those around her forward. She is not yet married, nor does she have any children. She can throw herself into her work however much she wants. She would travel to the various company sites, spending time building relationships and connecting with people every-where she goes. She loved her work and was darned good at it.

Having said that, Kelly shocked almost everyone when she announced she had decided to take a three-month summer sabbatical. Not a three-day weekend, but a three-month break. She went big! She left shortly thereafter to meet her youngest sister in South America. They backpacked, hiked, and went wherever their whims and feet took them. She witnessed catalysts in friends' lives around her, and she realized this was the time for her to prioritize herself. She was doubting a bit whether the path she was on was HER path, and she felt the time was perfect to go find herself. Her hope was not to simply wander around the globe but to use the change of scenery to change her perspective, look within and see what she might find.

I was so incredibly excited for her, yet selfishly I struggled with what to wish for my dear friend. Did I hope she would embrace a completely different life forever in Argentina or Peru, exploring all that life can offer her there? I feared never seeing my friend again. I had no idea when I could visit her in South America, and the time would fly by! Did I hope she would return all excited to double down on the trajectory she had been on? I then could enjoy the pleasure of her company on a more regular basis. What would she discover deep inside herself, and how would she change as a result?

All these emotions and questions swirled through my consciousness as she departed. I could not wait to find out who and what the new Kelly would be when I saw her next in person or via Skype from 5000 miles away. I admired her gumption to make this life decision and to pursue it with all her resources. She decided and shortly thereafter boarded a southbound plane at New York's Kennedy Airport.

When she returned, Kelly was a different person. Her core remained true, but she had brought back new perspective on her career and business life. Although she returned to the office for a few months to help push some critical projects over the finish line, her soul was no longer to be contained by the corporate parameters. She enrolled in graduate classes, passed her real estate exam, joined an entrepreneurial group, and set off on her own journey to re-imagine how real estate is transacted in the state of New York. Again – she just decided. It could have been so easy to pick up where she left off, yet she chose to take the uncertain path.

It is not *yet* the time for me to drop everything for a three-month sabbatical, because my life is at a different place right now. I can change my life, though through the decisions I make and the actions I take. I will let you in on a secret - you can too! Our boundaries are generally self-imposed, and our self-limiting beliefs slow us down more than any other externally imposed limitation. How are you going to reinvent your life and bring your dreams to reality? What indecision is standing in your way?

How often do we waste energy on the pointless agony of making a decision for which there is no wrong answer? A few years ago, an intern was trying to decide whether to join the multinational conglomerate he had enjoyed interning with or to go to Manhattan to become an investment banker. The IB role paid better, and everyone else in his class was gravitating there. He enjoyed the work he had been doing, though, and the company itself. His supervisor contemplated how best to counsel him.

It struck me that he was not faced with making any unalterable choices. Therefore, the best answer was to follow his heart. If he changed his mind later, there was nothing to keep him from reapplying to one of the investment banks a month, year, or decade later. On a bigger scale, with the notable exception of bringing a life into or out of this world or squandering time, are there any fundamentally irreversible decisions in life? You decide to move to California and hate it? Move somewhere else. You decide to marry someone and it does not work out? Get a divorce. You decide to take a job that turns out terrible? Quit and get a new job. You place a bet on an investment and change your mind? Cash out, or go find more money to make a different investment.

I am not suggesting that these decisions have no implications or repercussions, but simply that they are impermanent. Bringing a child into the world, or taking someone out of the world -

permanent. A day, year, or decade wasted - also permanent. Everything else is flexible. So take the chance on the option that most excites you with prospects for joy and fulfillment. Face your fear, listen to the song in your heart, and go for it.

I met a new friend not too long ago at a three-day conference. At the time of our meeting, she was at a crossroad of her own. Recently she left her prior company and now she was deciding between joining another one or starting her own venture. Branching out on her own was the more exciting option, but it carried with it a good deal of uncertainty. Tami and I connected and she quietly shared her story with me.

She had gone through some personal trials that led to deep panic attacks, sometimes of indescribable intensity. After a couple years of combating these attacks, she began to think the anxiety itself was literally going to kill her.

Finally, she reconciled with herself. She considered and recognized all of the blessings she had received in her life. She had been profoundly loved and extremely lucky, and she had achieved quite a bit. At this point, even the worst that could happen – premature death – was no longer terrible given these counter balances. Tami had a strong will to live and absolutely no desire to die, but she accepted that result if it was meant to be.

Miraculously, once she accepted this worst case possibility when facing a crisis, her anxiety smoothly evaporated. She realized that it was the uncertainty and the unknown driving all the stress, not the actual situation at hand. This way of thinking helped her to achieve peace and compassion for herself. The tool she needed to deal with scenarios of huge uncertainty lay within her. It allowed her to make decisions with incomplete information, in order to move forward.

At the end of the three-day conference, Tami pulled me aside with an epilogue. She had made the decision to go off and start her own venture. She was confident that she could always find employment another time with another company, but for now, she had to go on her own and try to start her own company. Her time is now, and she is leaning into the uncertainty.

Dislike your choice? Make a new one. The best that can happen is you find happiness and fulfillment beyond your wildest dreams. Take the unknown or scenic path, try new experiences, and do not be afraid to look like a fool along the way. Chances are you are the only one looking most of the time anyway. Your worst case scenario is seldom worse than you are today.

Identify what future unknowns are causing you stress and uncertainty today. What stands between you and making decisions? You cannot go back in time, and you cannot recover time that has been wasted. You can make the most of every minute from here on out by making decisions and taking the path with the most promise for your future. Let fear of the unknown go. What is the worst that can happen? If you can accept any of the likely outcomes, let the fear and anxiety go. If you cannot accept specific outcomes, then focus your risk mitigation efforts on ensuring that this outcome does not happen. Whatever you do, do not sit still in indecision. It is neither helping you move forward nor mitigating the risk of your undesired outcomes. People more often regret what they do NOT do as opposed to what they do.

If you do not get started today or this week or this year, then you will finish a day or week or year later, having done nothing if you ever get around to it at all. Make your plan, take the first few steps forward, and go into the uncertainty with a positive attitude and great expectations.

"When you finally decide, the fog will lift.
The clearing will open toward a new lens and landscape.
Deciding paves way for fresh space to pour through."

~ Victoria Erickson, Author

PRIME YOURSELF FOR SUCCESS EVERY MORNING

It never hurts to remind yourself of what it is you are trying to achieve. At the start of this year, I tried something new. On my morning commute, I decided to leverage my drive in a new way. I set my intentions and declared what my three key accomplishments would be for the day. Being the driver, I could not write anything down. Instead, I opened the voice memo app on my phone. I started talking to myself.

- The three things I needed to accomplish at work
- A renewed commitment to clean eating (Whole30)
- What time I would get into bed (9:45PM)
- How much water I would drink for the day (90 ounces)
- The time I would commit to exercise (20 minutes walking)
- A reminder to give more smiles
- My resolve to say nice things to at least three people.

I played it back three times over the car's sound system to embed it in my head then navigated into my parking spot.

I surprised myself by thinking about my commitments all day long. I corrected my behavior a few times when I noticed being drawn into the email backlog or social media. I accomplished all the goals I set except I forgot to smile more.

I had room for improvement. I could have done a bit more on one of the three work tasks and cut out the social media altogether during the workday. Regardless I was pleased with myself when I returned to my car and replayed my recording one final time. I repeated this again all week long and was amazed at how it changed my productivity and focus. This is one simple life hack to turn on your focus automatically.

There are many priming rituals that successful people enact. Tony Robbins is famous for his morning priming. He does this daily without fail, regardless of day of the week or where in the world he wakes up. It begins with a plunge into extreme cold. The goal is to drop his surface body temperature and simultaneously wake up the body and mind. The cold also reduces inflammation and triggers a rush of endorphins.

Once fully awakened by his sharp drop in temperature, Tony's ritual has three key components: deep breathing, expressing gratitude and sending positive thoughts into the universe for others. Instrumental music plays in the background. He requires no more than ten minutes to complete this ritual, and while small in investment, it sets up his entire day for success before enjoying a nutritious breakfast. Tony is one of the most recognized, influential, successful performance coaches in the world, and he knows what works for himself. He evangelizes it to others.

Another successful life coach I appreciate is Hal Elrod who has an incredible story of his own. Hit head-on by a drunk driver at the age of twenty, he was told that he would never walk again, and that he had permanent brain damage. He decided not to accept this fate. Hal trained his memory back to full functionality, and he not only learned again to walk but also went on to complete an ultra marathon. From this, he wrote his first book, *Taking Life Head On,*[51] and became a success coach.

When the great recession hit, his clients prioritized paying their mortgage over their success coach. His business tanked and again he was at the bottom. He had to overcome this setback in an extremely different way, with no doctors, nurses, or friends hovering by his bedside to help in his recovery. After languishing in an extended slump, he started researching what the most successful people do every day. He came up with his own morning success ritual. Hal's second book, *The Miracle Morning*[52] has now changed hundreds of thousands of lives worldwide. *The Miracle Morning* is taking on a life of its own and becoming a movement. As of mid-2018, he has twelve variations tailored to different audiences.

Hal's ritual is a combination of six practices, best performed in the morning, ideally over the course of an hour, though you can do both truncated and extended versions. His famous SAVERS are

Silence (or prayer or meditation), Affirmations, Visualization, Exercise, Reading, and Scribing (or writing or journaling). Hal has an online Facebook community that has over 175,000 members, which has more than tripled over the past eighteen months. It is the MOST positive corner of the Internet I have ever encountered in my life. Members share their successes, provide support to one another, and send both gratitude and cries for help into a listening world. I have not yet seen a single snarky post or comment within that group, and it continually amazes me. I know that when I am doing my SAVERS that my entire day goes better, regardless of whether I get up earlier than normal to do them. Other friends I have told about it experience the same benefits, and their successes are motivating me to recommit to my own morning routines. Success is contagious, and surrounding yourself with winners drives you to elevate your own game.

Once you have your plan in place, you have to hold yourself accountable to following through on it. At the start of each day, declare *to yourself* what it is you intend to accomplish. At the end of the day, objectively assess your day's achievements and how you feel about them. Savor your accomplishments, and express gratitude to the people and forces that benefited you. Set your intention for tomorrow, and get a great night's sleep. Tomorrow is another opportunity to go be awesome. Ultimate success is yours for the taking and the making.

"When you're grateful you can't be angry,
and when you're grateful you can't be fearful."

~ Tony Robbins, American author, entrepreneur,
philanthropist and life coach

PART 4: EXECUTION ACTION CHALLENGES

How Could I?:

1. Think about your own "I can'ts". Identify one example of something you have ruled out for yourself.
2. Reframe your language and see what opens up. For example, instead of reinforcing to yourself *"I can't retire early,"* challenge yourself with *"How could I retire early?"* and *"If I retired early, what would I do?"* Or instead of *"I can't afford to buy that house,"* ask yourself *"How can I afford to buy that house?"*
3. List out what you need, identify what you have, and look for creative ways to fill the remaining gaps.
   a. Do you need specific mad skills?
   b. More education, knowledge, or training?
   c. Specific people or their connections?
   d. Funding? Time?
4. Once you start identifying what you need, talk incessantly about it. Invite those resources into your life.

Set Micro Goals:

1. Revisit your top three Boulders. What is most important to you, at the big-picture level?
2. How can you break those down into smaller action plans of which you can achieve meaningful progress on a daily basis?
3. Set micro-goals, and accomplish them first in your day.
4. Identify nudges that may help you subconsciously make the choices you want to make

And ... GO!:

1. Make your decision then take a positive step toward that goal TODAY.
2. Set a micro-goal for today, whether it be researching how to do it online, talking to someone who is already doing it, or if you already know what you have to do – do it!

Savor the Victory:

1. Your masterpiece is ready and it is time to enjoy! Sit down and enjoy the delicious taste of victory. You have worked hard for this, overcoming obstacles and growing along the way. Celebrate!
2. As with many triumphs, take a moment of gratitude for all who had a part in getting you to where you are today.

PARTING THOUGHTS

I hope you have found one, two, or a dozen golden nuggets to incorporate into your own journey. Channel your inner water, and flow around, over, under, and through the rocks in your path. I DARE you to try something new starting today. Give it time and repetition to allow your improvement to take hold, then introduce a second improvement. You are worth the investment.

Review this book again in six months. Revisit the parts that caught your imagination. Try a third idea and a fourth. Give it a go!

We are each continual Do It Yourself works in progress from the day we are born until the day we die. It is up to each of us to decide which way to steer our boat - into the wind, with the current, or in a straight line to our destination. We each have the power of choice. Use your rudder with care. I wish the following for you:

1. Never stop dreaming in the first place. If I or anybody else claims you cannot do whatever it is you desire, figure out how it can be done, not why it cannot.

2. If you are getting pressure to do something out of alignment with your own path, stay faithful to yourself. You are sculpting your own life, and nobody else's.

3. Be willing to prioritize and sacrifice. You can do, be, and have anything you want. You may not be able to do, be, and

have it all simultaneously or immediately. By punting less important things, the pain of the sacrifice dissipates.

4. Bring others along with you in realizing your dreams. If those around you are unsupportive, assemble a new entourage. Share your time with winners who help you achieve your dreams. Help others achieve theirs.

5. Find the connections that exist everywhere at every level. Build relationships with other people. Honor how our internal systems are all interconnected. Care for the planet.

6. Live in the present. It is paradoxically infinitely small yet never-ending. Breathe in clean air. Exhale out stress and gratitude. Embrace today with your whole heart.

7. Have fun along the way! Celebrate wins large and small, and enjoy your annual scenic ride around the sun!

8. Be authentic, be tenacious!! Be you. If you are not going to be you, who else will?

I promise the best project you will ever work on is you. Here is to you and your own wild, raging success. Go with the flow and show those rocks who's boss!

Lastly, I have a personal request of you to help me achieve my own dream. If you found this book helpful, please tell a friend. Consider leaving a few helpful words on your favorite book review platform. My aspiration is to help as many others pursue and reach their own dreams as possible, and this is my way to share the love. Thank you for being a part of my story. With so much gratitude,

~ Brooke xoxox

ABOUT THE AUTHOR

Brooke married her high school crush and lives in Richmond, Virginia with the love of her life, their three young children, two cats, and a new rescue pup. She works in Corporate America by day, raises her family during nights and weekends, supports her husband's entrepreneurial ventures, and writes in her copious spare time. She is passionate about personal growth, holistic health, real estate, achieving financial independence, great food, and showing her children the world.

This is Brooke's first publication, with a grand plan to "10x it" with nine additional books to follow.

END NOTES

Chapter 1
[1] www.merriam-webster.com/dictionary/destination, Accessed July 8, 2018
[2] There is no endnote #2, other than to encourage you to smile!
[2] Ware, Bronnie. *The Top Five Regrets of the Dying: A Life Transformed by the Dearly Departing.* Hay House; Reprint edition (March 20, 2012).
[3] www.youtube.com/watch?v=ji5_MqicxSo, Accessed September 23, 2018.

Chapter 2
[4] Carroll, Lewis, 1832-1898. *Alice's Adventures in Wonderland.* Peterborough, Ont.: Broadview Press, 2000.
[5] Frankl, Viktor E. *Man's Search for Meaning: An Introduction to Logotherapy.* New York: Simon & Schuster, 1984. Print.
[6] Ferriss, Timothy. *The 4-Hour Work Week.* Random House, 2011.

Chapter 4
[7] www.merriam-webster.com/dictionary/attitude, Accessed July 8, 2018
[8] www.nba.com/history/players/jordan_bio.html Accessed July 8, 2018

Chapter 5
[9] blog.harveker.com/3-steps-overcome-fear/, Accessed July 8, 2018
[10] "Cabbage Patch Kids cause near Riots. Shoppers Queue Up for Dolls." The Victoria Advocate, Monday November 28, 1983, p. 2A.

Chapter 6
[11] TED.com. TED is a nonprofit devoted to spreading ideas, usually in the form of short, powerful talks (18 minutes or less). TED began in 1984 as a conference where Technology, Entertainment and Design converged, and today covers almost all topics — from science to business to global issues — in more than 100 languages.
[12] ayearofreadingtheworld.com/what-on-earth-am-i-doing/ Accessed July 8, 2018

Chapter 7
[13] Benson, Herbert, and Miriam Z. Klipper. *The Relaxation Response.* New York: Avon, 1975.
[14] Millman, Dan. *Way of the Peaceful Warrior: A Book That Changes Lives.* 2006.

Chapter 8
[15] www.merriam-webster.com/dictionary/resources, Accessed July 8, 2018
[16] www.nhi.fhwa.dot.gov/downloads/freebies/172/PR%20Pre-course%20Reading%20Assignment.pdf, Accessed July 8, 2018
[17] Gladwell, Malcolm, 1963-. *Outliers : The Story of Success.* New York: Little, Brown and Co., 2008.

Chapter 9

[18] https://chiefpeopleofficerusatodaynetwork.blogspot.com

[19] Formerly the American Society for Training and Development (ASTD). Study cited in uponly.co/2015/01/08/how-to-increase-the-odds-of-reaching-your-goals-by-85-2/ Accessed July 8, 2018, and www.mandyschumaker.com/how-to-double-your-success-rate/ Accessed July 8, 2018

[20] Health.clevelandclinic.org/2016/11/why-giving-is-good-for-your-health/, Accessed July 8, 2018

[21] Cialdini, Robert B. *Influence: The Psychology of Persuasion*. New York: HarperCollins, 1994.

[22] dental.washington.edu/wp-content/media/alumni/32067.DentalSpr03.pdf, Accessed July 8, 2018

[23] www.builtbygirls.com

[24] Pay It Forward. Screenplay by Leslie Dixon. Based on the book *Pay it Forward* by Catherine Ryan Hyde. Directed by Mimi Leder. Warner Brothers, 2000.

Chapter 10

[25] Isolation of a Central Bottleneck of Information Processing with Time-Resolved fMRI. Paul E. Dux, Jason Ivanoff, Christopher L. Asplund, and Rene´ Marois. Department of Psychology, Vanderbilt Vision Research Center Center for Integrative and Cognitive Neurosciences. Vanderbilt University, Nashville, Tennessee 37203. Neuron, ISSN: 0896-6273, Vol: 52, Issue: 6, Page: 1109-20. Publication Year: 2006

[26] Schmeichel, B. J. (2007). Attention control, memory updating, and emotion regulation temporarily reduce the capacity for executive control. *Journal of Experimental Psychology: General, 136*(2), 241-255.

[28] There is no endnote #28, just a thank you for reading this far.

[29] There is no endnote #29. Microsoft Word has added a few ghosts in the machine that I can no longer justify precious time toward debugging. Again, I offer you an extra smile!

[27] www.psychologytoday.com/blog/mental-wealth/201402/gray-matters-too-much-screen-time-damages-the-brain, Accessed July 8, 2018

[28] www.aap.org/en-us/about-the-aap/aap-press-room/pages/american-academy-of-pediatrics-announces-new-recommendations-for-childrens-media-use.aspx, Accessed July 8, 2018

[29] www.youtube.com/results?search_query=agile+family

Chapter 11

[30] Carcinogenicity of shift-work, painting, and fire-fighting. *Straif K, Baan R, Grosse Y, Secretan B, El Ghissassi F, Bouvard V, Altieri A, Benbrahim-Tallaa L, Cogliano V, WHO International Agency For Research on Cancer Monograph Working Group. Lancet Oncol. 2007 Dec; 8(12):1065-6.*

[31] Erren, Thomas C et al. "Shift Work and Cancer: The Evidence and the Challenge." *Deutsches Ärzteblatt International* 107.38 (2010): 657–662. PMC. Web. 18 Sept. 2017.

[32] Behavioural Brain Research 69 (1995) 55-63. Research report: Sleep deprivation in the rat by the disk-over-water method by Allan Rechtschaffen, Bernard M. Bergmann. Accepted 1 December 1995

[33] theshawnstevensonmodel.com, Accessed July 8, 2018

[34] Stevenson, Shawn. *Sleep Smarter: 21 Essential Strategies to Sleep Your Way to a Better Body, Better Health, and Bigger Success.* Rodale Books, 2016.

[35] www.forbes.com/sites/travisbradberry/2012/08/21/caffeine-the-silent-killer-of-emotional-intelligence/#2ca75cff118c

36 "First Control of Fire by Human Beings—How Early?" www.beyondveg.com/nicholson-w/hb/hb-interview2c.shtml. Accessed September 22, 2018.

Chapter 12
37 www.merriam-webster.com/dictionary/execution, Accessed July 8, 2018
38 World Wide Opportunities on Organic Farms, or Willing Workers on Organic Farms
39 Enchanted. By Bill Kelly. Dir. Kevin Lima. Perf. Timothy Spall James Marsden. Walt Disney Pictures. 2007.

Chapter 13
40 Duhigg, Charles. *The Power of Habit: Why We Do What We Do in Life And Business.* New York: Random House, 2012.

Chapter 14
41 Fincher, David, Scott Rudin, Dana Brunetti, Luca M. De, Ceán Chaffin, Aaron Sorkin, Jeff Cronenweth, Jacqueline West, Ren Klyce, Donald G. Burt, Trent Reznor, Atticus Ross, Kevin Spacey, Jesse Eisenberg, Andrew Garfield, Justin Timberlake, Armie Hammer, Max Minghella, Josh Pence, Brenda Song, Rashida Jones, John Getz, David Selby, Denise Grayson, Douglas Urbanski, Rooney Mara, and Ben Mezrich. *The Social Network.* Culver City, California: Sony Pictures Home Entertainment, 2011.
42 Kaplan, Robert S, and David P. Norton. *The Balanced Scorecard: Translating Strategy into Action.* Boston: Harvard Business School Press, 1996.
43 Thaler, Richard H, and Cass R. Sunstein. *Nudge: Improving Decisions About Health, Wealth, and Happiness.* New Haven: Yale University Press, 2008.
44 Van Kleef E, Shimizu M, Wansink B. Serving Bowl Selection Biases the Amount of Food Served. J Nutr Educ Behav. 2012; 44:66–70.
45 Stroebele N, Ogden LG, Hill JO. Do calorie-controlled portion sizes of snacks reduce energy intake? Appetite. 2009; 52:793–96.
46 Arno, Anneliese, and Steve Thomas. "The Efficacy of Nudge Theory Strategies in Influencing Adult Dietary Behaviour: A Systematic Review and Meta-Analysis." BMC Public Health 16 (2016): 676. PMC. Web. 28 May 2018.
47 Bodor JN, Rose D, Farley TA, Swalm C, Scott SK. Neighbourhood Fruit and Vegetable Availability and Consumption: The Role of Small Food Stores in an Urban Environment. Public Health Nutr. 2008;11:413–20.
48 Institutional.vanguard.com/iam/pdf/CRRATEP_AutoEnrollDefault.pdf, Accessed July 8, 2018.
49 Whole30.com, Accessed July 8, 2018
50 Hartwig, Dallas and Melissa Hartwig. *It Starts With Food.* Las Vegas: Victory Belt Publishing, Inc., 2014.
51 Elrod, Hal. *Taking Life Head On! (The Hal Elrod Story): How To Love The Life You Have While You Create The Life of Your Dreams.* Hal Elrod, 2012.
52 Elrod, Hal. *The Miracle Morning: The Not-so-Obvious Secret Guaranteed to Transform Your Life Before 8am.* 1st Paperback Edition. Hal Elrod, 2012.

Made in the USA
Columbia, SC
25 April 2019